Edward Choppee Mitchell, Law Academy of Philadelphia

The Equitable Relations of Buyer and Seller of Land Under Contract and Before Conveyance

Edward Choppee Mitchell, Law Academy of Philadelphia

The Equitable Relations of Buyer and Seller of Land Under Contract and Before Conveyance

ISBN/EAN: 9783744670463

Printed in Europe, USA, Canada, Australia, Japan

Cover: Foto ©ninafisch / pixelio.de

More available books at **www.hansebooks.com**

THE

EQUITABLE RELATIONS

OF

BUYER AND SELLER OF LAND

UNDER CONTRACT AND BEFORE CONVEYANCE

TWO LECTURES BEFORE THE LAW ACADEMY OF PHILADELPHIA

BY

E. COPPÉE MITCHELL

PHILADELPHIA
REES WELSH & CO
LAW BOOKSELLERS AND PUBLISHERS
N. W. CORNER OF SIXTH AND WALNUT STREETS
1877

It is thought proper to explain that the following Lectures were prepared for the Law Academy of Philadelphia, and were delivered before the Academy, in April, 1877. They are printed as originally written, without material change. The publication of them was not contemplated, but was afterwards suggested.

PHILADELPHIA, *May* 9, 1877.

CONTENTS.

	PAGE
SPECIFIC PERFORMANCE, General principles,	5– 8
I.—REQUISITES OF CONTRACT,	9–20
British Statute of Frauds,	9
Pennsylvania Statute of Frauds,	11
Who must sign Contract,	12
Form of Contract,	13–17
No words of Inheritance necessary,	16
Part Performance,	17–20
Change of Possession indispensable,	19
II.—EFFECT OF CONTRACT,	21–25
Equitable Conversion, general doctrine,	21
Same applied to Contract of Sale,	23
Title of Vendee after Contract,	24
Title of Vendor after Contract,	24
III.—EFFECT OF LIENS,	26–43
Liens prior to Contract,	26
Lien created by Contract, Vendor's Lien,	26–34
English doctrine not adopted,	28
Express Contract for lien, after Conveyance,	29
Lien before Conveyance,	33
Liens Subsequent to Contract,	35–43
Judgments against Vendor,	35
Attachment execution will not lie,	36
This rule compared with other cases,	37

CONTENTS.

	PAGE.
Ejectment by Vendor,	38
Sheriff's sale of Vendor's title,	39
Judgments against Vendee,	39
Effect of Merger on Liens,	40

IV.—EFFECT OF SHERIFF'S SALE,   44– 8
Sale on Lien prior to Contract,   44
Sale on Proceeding for Purchase Money,   46
Sale on Judgment against Vendor,   47
Sale on Judgment against Vendee,   48

V.—REMEDY UPON CONTRACT,   49–82
Remedy by Bill in Equity,   49–66
What must be shown,   49
Dower—Where wife of Vendor refuses,   50
Mutuality,   53
Marketable Title,   54
Compensation,   55
Time not material in Equity,   56
Bill against purchaser,   57–66
Difference between English doctrine and ours,   62
When Bill against Purchaser may be maintained,   65
Equitable Ejectment,   66–74
Substitute for Bill,   67
Functions of Judge and Jury,   68
Conditional Verdict,   70
One judgment enough,   71
Action at law on the Contract,   74–81
Measure of Damages,   74
Damages against Vendor,   74
Damages on Verbal Contract,   76
Damages against Vendee,   79
Interest on Purchase Money,   80
Statute of Limitations,   81

CONTRACTS FOR THE SALE OF LAND.

Contracts for the sale of real property differ from other contracts, chiefly from two causes. One is the Statute of Frauds, requiring a writing signed by the party, or his authorized agent, to bind the bargain. The other is to be found in the peculiar doctrines of the Courts of Equity, according to which they have been accustomed to enforce or refuse specific performance of such contracts by the parties bound by them.

Of the Statute of Frauds I shall have something to say presently. Let me direct your attention for a few minutes, by way of introduction, to the general principles of specific performance.

SPECIFIC PERFORMANCE.—Perhaps there is no one of the many differences between the two systems of law and equity that is more marked than that which exists in their methods of dealing with breaches of contract. Of course it is not every contract that comes within equitable jurisdiction. A chancellor does not interfere with his extraordinary power unless there is a want of sufficient remedy otherwise, which would result in a complete or partial failure of justice. But when the proper case does arise, upon a breach or threatened breach of contract, the relief afforded is as nearly perfect as can be. The decree is that the contract shall be performed as it was made; that the party shall do exactly what he promised to do, and what the one who dealt with him had a right to expect him to do.

The common law almost uniformly gives redress for breach of contract by compensation in money. The remedy of the injured party is confined to the recovery of damages in an action. That is in effect giving to every one, bound by a contract, the choice either to keep the contract, or break it and pay damages. If he would rather pay than stick to his bargain, there is nothing to prevent his doing so.

The difference, I may say, is not in principle so much as in the remedy. It is just as clearly well settled at law as in equity that one who makes a contract is bound to perform it; but the law says to such an one, "pay damages if you do not choose to keep your agreement," while equity gives him no choice whatever, and says, "you shall perform your contract, or be severely punished for disobedience."

While it was not every contract which would entitle an injured party to seek relief in equity, it has long been well settled that every contract *for the sale of land* will, if valid and fair in other respects, be enforced by a decree of specific performance. The idea which underlies the equitable jurisdiction is, that there are some cases in which the damages resulting from a breach of contract can be accurately measured and amply compensated by the recovery of a sum of money—and wherever that is true the law affords a sufficient remedy. While in other cases an action for damages is wholly inadequate for the purposes of justice, either because the subject of the contract is intended for some special purpose of use or enjoyment, which can only be satisfied by having the individual thing itself; or because the measure of damage is uncertain and cannot be ascertained with accuracy, and therefore the verdict of a jury could not do complete justice. As Lord Macclesfield said in the leading case of *Cuddee* v. *Rutter*,[1] which was on a bill to enforce specific performance of a contract to transfer South Sea stock: "There was no reason to bring "a bill for specific performance of this agreement, "because there is no difference between this £1000 "South Sea stock and another £1000 stock, which "the plaintiff might have bought of any other person "on the same day. And the plaintiff does not "suffer at all by the non-performance of the agree- "ment specifically, if the defendant pays him the "difference. * * * This differs very much from "the case of a contract for lands—some lands "being more valuable than others, at least more "convenient than others to the purchaser; but

---

[1] 1 P. Wms. 570. (1 Ldg. Cas. in Equity, *640.)

"there is no difference in stock—one man's stock is of equal benefit or conveniency as another's."

The ruling in this case has been fully adopted in Pennsylvania, and the chancery doctrines respecting contracts for the sale of land have been uniformly enforced by our courts, through common law forms when we had no Courts of Equity, and since then in regular equity modes of proceeding. There has been, however, this peculiarity with respect to the Pennsylvania law on this subject; that from 1736 to 1836, a period of exactly one hundred years, we had no courts of general equity jurisdiction, and although equity principles were part of the common law of Pennsylvania, they were necessarily enforced by means of common law forms, and this circumstance has given rise to many peculiarities in the doctrines concerning sales of land, which it will be part of my duty in these lectures to explain and illustrate.

I propose to consider, *first*, the requisites of the contract; *second*, the effect and consequences of the contract; *third*, the effect of liens against the vendor and vendee respectively; *fourth*, the effect of a sheriff's sale of the land which has been articled, to use the phrase of the report books; and *fifth* and *last*, the remedy on the contract, by the vendor against the vendee, the vendee against the vendor, and the measure of damages when an action at law is brought for its breach.

1. THE REQUISITES OF THE CONTRACT.

Except the provisions of the Statute of Frauds, there is little to distinguish a contract for the sale of land from any other contract of sale in this respect. The same rules apply as to certainty, actual fraud, consideration, capacity and consent.

STATUTE OF FRAUDS.—The Statute of Frauds, as I have said, makes a marked difference between a contract for the sale of land and any other contract of sale; and not to weary you with a recitation of the provisions of the statute in detail, let me summarize them so far as this subject is concerned, by saying that they require every such contract of sale to be by deed or note in writing, signed by the party to be charged therewith, or by his agent thereto lawfully authorized in writing; and that no estate or interest in the land can be otherwise created, assigned, or transferred, except by act or operation of law. The words "by act or operation of law," of course, refer to cases of "resulting" and "constructive" trusts, which need not occupy us now.

In all the systems of law of which we have any knowledge, the transfer of title to land has been a subject of grave importance, and solemnities and sanctions were required, which were not thrown around the transfer of title to personal property. From the first recorded purchase of land, by Abraham from the sons of Heth, of the cave of Macpelah, where he buried Sarah, his wife, down to the present time, the common consent of mankind has demanded that the evidence of contracts for the sale of real estate should be of a character which could be preserved, and have something of the permanency of the subject that was dealt with. "And Abraham spoke unto Ephron in the audience of the people of the land," says the sacred Writing; and after the terms of the bargain are carefully recorded in the Book of Genesis, we have this conclusion, "and the field of Ephron, and the cave which was therein, and all the trees that were in the field and that were in all the borders round about, were made sure unto Abraham for a possession, in the presence of the children of Heth, before all that went in at the gate of his city." And so throughout the history of the Jews, of Greece, and Rome, and among our own ancestors, from whose feudal system we have derived our own system of land tenure, there have been always required some solemnities more than were necessary in a bargain about a chattel. The audience at the gate of the city; the shoe plucked off; the feudal investiture; the livery of seisin; the fealty, homage and attornment in the lord's court; all of these, and others in turn, according to the civilization and development of the society which practiced them, marked the same idea; that the evidence of the transfer of title to land was to be permanent, certain and notorious; and in our day we have in their place, to express precisely the same idea, and to illustrate precisely the same principle, the Statute of Frauds, which requires a writing, and the recording acts, which require the deed to be put on record within a reasonable time after it is made; so that the evidence of a contract respecting land may not depend upon fallible and perishable human memory, or remain secret, beyond the knowledge of those who by subsequent dealings may be brought within its influence.

THE PENNSYLVANIA STATUTE. — Our Statute of Frauds was adopted March 21st, 1772, and is condensed from portions of the British Statute of 29 Car. II, c. 3, consequently the English decisions upon that statute have had a great effect in moulding the law of Pennsylvania, and deciding what our own construction of our statute should be. A notable circumstance is that the fourth section of the British Statute was not adopted in Pennsylvania. That section provides that no *action* shall be brought to charge any person upon any contract or sale of land, or any interest in or concerning land, unless the agreement shall be in writing, and signed by the party or his lawfully authorized agent. It was, as I said, left out of the act of 1772, but was enacted as the fifth section of our Act of Assembly of April 22d, 1856, and remained in force for one year, when it was repealed by the act of May 13th, 1857, Pamph. Laws, 500.

Owing to the fact that this section is not in force, it cannot be said that a verbal contract for the sale of lands is totally void in Pennsylvania, as it is in England under their statute; because here an action may be brought and maintained for a breach of contract for the sale of land which is entirely by word of mouth. The courts, however, have been very careful so to instruct the juries as to the measure of damages in such actions that they cannot be used to enforce specific performance of the contract, or to accomplish any result which would be equivalent to it. The measure of damages in such an action, therefore, under no circumstances includes compensation for the loss of the bargain; and one who sues upon a verbal contract for the sale of land, can recover nothing but the purchase money which he has paid, interest upon it, and any special damage which he has suffered by reason of the non-performance of the contract, such as the preparation of title papers, the employment of counsel, &c. But of this another time.

Who Must Sign.—The first point to which I will call your attention under this statute is, that only the person who is to be charged by the contract is required to sign it. The vendor who is selling land, and whose title is to be affected by the contract, cannot be bound unless the contract is in writing and signed by him. The vendee who is not dealing with title to land, but who is only making a contract to part with a sum of money, is not within the protection of the statute, and he may be bound by a verbal promise. It is sufficient if he accepts the contract without signing it. Let me illustrate this: In a case where the agreement in question was signed only by the vendors, they left it optional with the vendee to take the land within ten days upon the terms proposed, which were fully stated. The vendee gave them notice, within the time, *verbally*, that he would take the land, and the Supreme Court held that the agreement was good under the statute, both parties being bound by it.[1] But, of course, no contract is binding upon one party unless it is binding upon both, and if a verbal contract for the sale of land be made it cannot be enforced by either party; the statute forbids the vendor to be bound by it, and the vendee cannot be bound because there is no mutuality. A contract ought to be the source of mutual obligation and mutual remedy. It would be against all our ideas of justice that a man who is not bound by a contract, may yet be able to say to the other party, "you shall be bound by the same contract, and while I may keep it or not as I please, you shall keep it whether you choose or not."[2]

THE FORM OF THE CONTRACT.—The writing required by the statute may be either a deed or note. Such are its express terms. No form of words is

---

[1] *Smith & Fleck's Appeal,* 19 P. F. Sm. 474.
[2] *Wilson* v. *Clarke,* 1 W. & S. 554; *Bodine* v. *Glading,* 9 H. 50.

necessary. The statute requires no seal; only that it should be signed. Consequently it has been well settled that any memorandum signed by the party, which contains the necessary elements of a contract, is sufficient—a receipt—a letter—a bond. In *Colt v. Selden*,[1] the note in writing, which was held sufficient, was in the form of a letter from the purchaser offering to buy the land, with an endorsement of acceptance on the back of it signed by the owner of the land. It is only necessary that the memorandum in writing, whatever it is, should be so precise as to enable an inquirer to ascertain the terms of the contract, the price, and the land to be conveyed. So much, however, *is* necessary. It is not sufficient if any essential part of the contract remains to be proved by parol. In one case the writing was in the form of a receipt for part payment of the purchase money of a piece of land, and it was held not sufficient because the total amount of the price to be paid was not mentioned.[2] In another case, the contract contained everything but a sufficient identification of the land which was meant to be sold, and it was held insufficient—without that, there was no contract.[3] It was once doubted, and there were conflicting decisions upon the question, whether the writing must be directly between the parties or their agents, but it was finally held that it must be so; otherwise, it would not be a con-

---

[1] 5 Watts, 525.   [2] *Soles* v. *Hickman*, 8 Harris, 181.
[3] *Ferguson* v. *Staver*, 9 Casey, 411.

tract, but rather an admission or recital of a contract made to a stranger.[1] In the case referred to, a recital in a deed was the note in writing that was supposed to be sufficient to take the case out of the statute, but the court held that this was no contract at all, but a simple recital between the defendant and a stranger.

But in this connection we must remember the maxim "that is certain which can be made certain." It is sufficient if the subject matter be identified in such a way as to show clearly what was meant; as, for instance, if a lot of land be referred to by a number on a plan, it is a sufficient description;[2] or be mentioned as contained in a certain survey.[3] And in one case the court ordered a surveyor to lay out the land contracted to be sold, for their information, and then decreed specific performance according to his report. The Supreme Court, on appeal, said that this course was eminently proper, and affirmed the decree.[4]

In short, the note in writing required by the statute, although it may be in any form, must yet contain all the essential elements of a contract of sale. It must describe the land with certainty, name the price to be paid, the time and terms of payment, and the parties who make it. If it comes up to this standard, it is sufficient. If it falls short, it is not.

---

[1] *Allen v. Allen,* 9 Wright, 468. [2] *Robinson v. Meyer,* 17 P. F. Smith, 9.
[3] *Armstrong v. Boyd,* 3 Penna. 458. [4] *Herdic's Appeal,* 8 P. F. Smith, 211.

No words of Inheritance Necessary.—Another equitable doctrine with respect to such contracts, relaxed the rigor of the common law in requiring words of inheritance to pass an estate in fee. Where the agreement is executory, looking to further deeds for its consummation between the parties, equity will presume that an estate in fee simple was meant to be transferred, from the circumstance that the price to be paid warrants such an inference.[1]

It is very important, therefore, in this connection, to note the distinction between an executory and an executed contract, for this equitable doctrine applies to one and not to the other. The case in our books, which perhaps most thoroughly illustrates this distinction, is one that we would hardly have expected to find, being upon an instrument drawn by a lawyer to secure payment of a contingent fee. He brought ejectment for a tract of land, and took an agreement from the plaintiffs that he was to receive as his fee one-sixth of the land in controversy, or of so much as should be recovered in the suit. If nothing was recovered he was to charge nothing for his services. In writing his agreement, however, although he made it very short and informal, he used the words "grant, bargain and sell," the ordinary words of a conveyance, and the court held that it was an executed contract,

---

[1] *McFarson's Appeal*, 1 Jones, 511; *Ogden* v. *Brown*, 9 Casey, 247; *Gaule* v. *Bilyeau*, 1 Casey, 521.

looking to no further conveyance between the parties, and there being no words of inheritance, the successful counsel took but a life estate in *his* one-sixth.[1]

EXCEPTIONS TO THE STATUTE — PART PERFORMANCE.—But the chief equitable exception to the statute is to be found in cases of what is technically called "*part performance;*" that is, where the contract, although verbal, has been so far performed that it would be a fraud upon the purchaser if it were not fully carried out.

It must be borne in mind that Courts of Equity are bound by statutes, and do not pretend to be at liberty to disregard them. But it is equally certain that they do interfere and give protection in some cases which are clearly within the letter of the Statute of Frauds; and they do this expressly on the ground that they will not allow the statute made to prevent frauds, by a too close adherence to its letter, to be made the means of executing a fraud, in total disregard and violation of its spirit. Consequently these equitable exceptions to the statute have been long well established in England,[2] and closely followed by our courts in this country. The Legislature of Pennsylvania has recognized this exception to the Statute of Frauds, and has defined what "part performance" is, in reference to con-

---
[1] *Gray* v. *Packer,* 4 W. & S. 17.
[2] *Ungley* v. *Ungley,* L. R., 4 Ch. Div. 73.

tracts for the sale of lands, made by persons who afterwards die. By the act of March 10th, 1818, Sect. 1, provision is made for enforcing a parol contract for the sale of land, made by an owner who afterwards dies, and then comes the definition I speak of—" In cases where such contracts shall have been so far in part executed as to render it unjust to rescind the same."

But the subject is worth a more careful consideration. It was formerly thought that a payment of the whole, or a considerable part of the purchase money, or giving security for it, was such a part performance as to take a contract for the sale of land out of the operation of the statute; but that doctrine has been finally overthrown. The mere payment of money can be compensated, and it is therefore no irreparable injury to the purchaser to enforce the statute; for nothing is to be considered a part performance which does not put the purchaser into a situation which will make it a fraud on him, unless the contract shall be enforced. There are many ingredients of more or less weight in making up part performance, but the chief and essential one is possession—*a change of possession in pursuance of the contract.* Where this element exists, the courts may or may not say that the contract has been part performed, but, without it, under any other circumstances, the statute is invariably enforced.[1] I do not mean to be under-

---

[1] *Robertson* v. *Robertson*, 9 Watts, 41.

stood as saying that a change of possession, standing entirely alone, is sufficient. That has been expressly decided not to be law. The bare loss of possession, it is said by the court, can be compensated, and consequently cannot be a sufficient part performance under the equity doctrine.[1]

But where there has been a change of possession *and* other circumstances, such as payment of a part of the price, it has been invariably held that the sale is good without a writing.[2] The possession, however, *must change.* A continued possession will not suffice. It is said that the law looks upon the change of the possession as in a sense equivalent to the writing which the statute requires—as evidence of the bargain substantially as good as could be afforded by the writing, and, therefore, there must be the publicity which attends an open transfer. So it was held in *Hill* v. *Myers*,[3] that one tenant in common in possession could not sell by parol to his co-tenant in possession, because there was no *change* in pursuance of the contract. Again, the change must be *in pursuance of the contract,* and, therefore, it follows that it must be made *after* the contract is made, and in execution of it.[4] Again, the possession must be *exclusive;* nothing else would have the effect of notoriety which is required, and this must be such as to notify the neighbors

---

[1] *Galbraith* v. *Galbraith,* 5 Watts, 146; *Dougan* v. *Blocker,* 12 Harris, 28; *Moore* v. *Small,* 7 Harris, 467. [2] *Millikin* v. *Dravo,* 17 P. F. Sm. 233.
[3] 7 Wright, 170. [4] *Aiken* v. *Young,* 2 Jones, 15.

that a change has taken place. Once more, the possession taken under the agreement must be *coextensive with the purchase.* Thus, in a contract for the sale of two pieces of land, possession was taken of but one, and it was held that the contract was not so far performed as to take the case out of the ban of the statute.[1] And lastly, an express contract must be clearly proved. All the essential elements of a contract must be affirmatively shown by direct evidence, and not by proof of facts from which an implied contract might be inferred. It must further appear that it was fair and conscionable, founded in sufficient consideration, and so far executed that it would be a fraud on the vendee not to fully perform it. Whether that has been done or not in any case is a question of *law* for the court, and it is error for a judge to submit it as a question of fact to be passed upon by a jury.[2]

There are other exceptions to the Statute of Frauds, such as judicial sales, &c., which are foreign to the subject of these lectures.

[1] *Allen's Estate*, 1 W. & S. 383.
[2] *Overmeyer* v. *Koerner*, 2 Weekly Notes, 6.

11. THE EFFECT AND CONSEQUENCES OF THE CONTRACT.

Suppose a complete, valid, and binding contract is made. Then it is that the equitable doctrine entirely changes the relations of the parties from what they would be at common law. At law, the vendor is the owner of the land as well and the same after the agreement as before. He is only personally bound by a contract, the breach of which will expose him to an action for damages. All the legal consequences of ownership attend his title. At his death it descends to his heir. The vendee has nothing but a *chose in action*—a right to bring an action for damages against the vendor if he should choose not to perform the agreement. He has no title to the land whatever and no estate or interest in it. In equity, however, all this is different. The doctrine of equitable conversion comes into play and entirely changes the relations of the parties from what they are at law.

EQUITABLE CONVERSION.—It may not be out of place here to state to you, briefly, the doctrine of equitable conversion, before applying it to the subject in hand. As I said before, equitable conversion is a fiction. Actual conversion, which is the same as to say *legal* conversion, is a change of property from real to personal, or from personal to real. If a man has money and buys land with it, he converts his personalty into real estate, and *vice versa*, a conversion is made where one who has land, sells it and gets money for it. The consequences of such an actual conversion are important. It makes a material difference in many respects whether the property which a man has, is real or personal; and of this any number of familiar illustrations might be given. The two species of property are regulated by different laws as to ownership and transfer. They occupy different positions with respect to claims of creditors and others, and on the death of the owner they descend to, or devolve upon, different persons, according to different rules. Equitable conversion is not actual, but imaginary. And by means of this fiction, in certain cases, and for the accomplishment of certain purposes, equity clothes real estate with all the. incidents of personalty, and personalty with all the incidents of real estate. The doctrine is founded upon the maxim that "equity considers that as done which ought to be done." This means simply, in this connection, that the rights of one man shall not be affected or impaired by the failure of another man to do his duty; and as applied to the conversion of property from real to personal, or from personal to real, the maxim reaches this result: that wherever it is the duty of any man thus to convert property, and the rights of other persons depend upon the performance or non-performance of that duty by him, for the sake of protecting and preserving those rights, equity will treat the property as if actually converted. Of course, if there be actual conversion there is no need for the interposition of the equitable doctrine, for then that which ought to be done has been done. It is only where there has been no actual conversion that the doctrine applies, for, I repeat, equitable conversion is an imaginary conversion.

Under this doctrine, in equity, the vendee is considered as the owner of the land,—as Judge Duncan said in an early case, "When a contract is made for " the sale of land, equity considers the vendee as the " owner of the estate sold, and the purchaser as a " trustee for the vendor for the purchase money. So " much is the vendee considered in contemplation of " equity, as actually seized of the estate, that he must " bear any loss which may happen to the estate " between the agreement and the conveyance, and he " will be entitled to any benefit which may accrue to " it in the interval, because by the contract he is the " owner of the premises to every intent and purpose " in equity."[1] The interest of the purchaser, then, after the bargain is made, is an estate in land which will descend to his heirs. It is not affected by the payment or non-payment of the purchase money. He is by mere force of the contract the owner of the whole estate, encumbered only by the balance of the purchase money due:[2]—and all the consequences of this

[1] *Richter v. Selin*, 8 S. & R. 439.   [2] *Siter's Appeal*, 2 Casey, 178.

doctrine are followed to their logical conclusion, except as to lien creditors, as will be hereafter stated.

The title of a vendor in equity is that of a trustee. His beneficial interest is a right to a sum of money, for which, before conveyance, he has a lien upon the land, and there is little to distinguish his possession in view of a court of equity, from that of a mortgagee. He holds the title as a security for the payment of the balance of the purchase money due, and when that is paid he must convey it. Upon his death the right to the money goes to his personal representatives as a chattel, and under our statutes for enforcing the contracts of decedents, the executors or administrators are required, after the contract has been duly proved to the court, to make a deed for the land to the purchaser upon payment of the balance of the price.

If the purchaser be in possession under the terms of the contract, as happens very frequently in some of the other counties in this State, he is bound to do nothing which will diminish the security of the vendor for the payment of the purchase money, and so he may be restrained from cutting timber upon the land if that will lessen its value.[1] But this is no more than will be done to any mortgagor, who, by such conduct, lessens the security of his creditor for the money charged upon the title. And his ownership of the land is not to be called in question from this circumstance, because it has been held, that although the

---

[1] *Coomalt* v. *Stanley*, 3 Clark's L. J. Rep. 389.

agreement expressly stipulate that no timber shall be cut until the land is paid for, yet the purchaser has an interest in the timber which he may transfer, and his vendee may maintain an action for injury to it, although he has no right to take it away from the land until the condition is complied with.[1] Indeed, so far has this equitable doctrine been carried under our peculiar system of administering equity in Pennsylvania through common law forms, that it has been determined that where a vendee of an undivided interest in land, was entitled according to his agreement to possession, he might maintain an action of *partition* against the co-tenant in common of his vendor.[2]

I have said that on the death of the vendee his title descends to his heirs. Of course, this circumstance would not deprive the vendor of his lien for the payment of the purchase money, but the purchase money was a debt due by the deceased vendee, and consequently it is payable out of his estate; and it has been determined, that if before conveyance he devised the land, although the contract calls for payment at a future day, the devisee will be entitled to have the estate paid for out of the personal property of his testator.[3]

---

[1] *Lillybridge* v. *Sartwell*, 8 Barr, 523.
[2] *Longwell* v. *Bently*, 11 Harris, 99.
[3] *Broom* v. *Monk*, 10 Vesey, 597; 3 Johns. Ch. 316.

III. THE EFFECT OF LIENS AGAINST VENDOR AND VENDEE RESPECTIVELY.

LIENS PRIOR TO THE CONTRACT.—Of course, those liens of every kind, by mortgage, judgment, or otherwise, which bind the land at the time the contract of sale is made, continue unaffected by the contract. As to them there is no equitable conversion whatever. Equitable conversion is a fiction—an imaginary conversion—which is introduced for the accomplishment of some equitable purpose, and which is kept up only for the accomplishment of that purpose. But if a man buys land which he knows (or ought to know) is subject to a mortgage or judgment lien, he takes it *cum onere*, and neither buyer nor seller can justly complain, if the enforcement of the lien creditor's legal rights deprives them of title. Consequently, a sheriff's sale under a lien which attached prior to the contract, passes both the legal and equitable estate in the law, and the sheriff's vendee takes it clear of the claims arising under the contract.

LIEN CREATED BY THE CONTRACT.—VENDOR'S LIEN.— The contract itself is the source of another lien, which attaches upon the equitable estate of the purchaser. And that is the *vendor's lien for the purchase money*, or so much of it as may remain unpaid. But this must not be confounded with what is called "vendor's lien," in the English equity books, for it is an entirely different thing. It is the well settled doctrine of the Court of Chancery in England, that the vendor of land has, even after he has made a formal, legal conveyance of the title, a lien for the amount of the purchase money remaining unpaid, not only as against the vendee himself and his heirs, but also against all subsequent purchasers and mortgagees, who took with notice that the purchase money remained unpaid. As Lord Eldon said in *Mackreth* v. *Symmons*,[1] "Where "the vendor conveys, without more, though the con- "sideration is upon the face of the instrument ex- "pressed to be paid, and by a receipt endorsed upon "the back; if it is a simple case of a conveyance, the "money, or part of it, not being paid, as between the "vendor and the vendee, and persons claiming as "volunteers, upon the doctrine of this court, (which "when it is settled has the effect of contract, though "perhaps no actual contract has taken place) a lien "shall prevail; in the one case for the whole consider- "ation, in the other, for that part of the money which "was not paid." This, he said, was the settled doctrine of the court, and then, after remarking upon the authorities, he added: "I cannot doubt that a person, "having got the estate of another, shall not, as "between them, keep it, and not pay the considera- "tion; and I have no doubt but that a third person, "having full knowledge that the other got the estate "without payment, ought not to be permitted to keep "it without making such payment."

[1] 15 Ves. 329.

This English doctrine was never adopted in Pennsylvania, but was expressly repudiated the first time the question was fairly raised in the Supreme Court. In the opinions of Judges Gibson and Duncan in this case,[1] which is a leading one in this State, it is clearly shown that the early settlers of the province did not bring this doctrine with them from England, for it has grown up there since the founding of the colony; that it was opposed to the spirit and policy of our legislation, which seeks to make all liens upon land the subjects of record; and that the doctrine accorded neither with the sentiments of the profession nor with the popular understanding.

It is owing to this difference between our system and the English, that the same deductions cannot be made from circumstances very nearly or entirely alike. If, as was formerly the custom in England, the possession of the title papers be looked upon as a distinguishing and almost an indispensable badge of a good title, so that the want of them is notice to a vendee that puts him upon inquiry as to the rights of a third person who may be in possession of them, then it might be fair to say that a deposit of title papers as security for a loan should create a valid mortgage, or that a complete deed, with a receipt for the purchase money appended or endorsed, would be insufficient to persuade an intending purchaser that his vendor's

---

[1] *Kauffelt v. Bower*, 7 S. & R. 63.

land was free from entanglements. But as a general rule, we have, by our Acts of Assembly, given to an intending purchaser of land, an unerring guide to an unencumbered title ; and where an absolute conveyance, free from all encumbrance, is found on record, and the records show no liens duly entered according to law, the buyer is safe in taking the title and paying for it.[1]

EXPRESS CONTRACT MAY BE MADE FOR LIEN.—Of course, the parties may contract that there shall be a lien, notwithstanding the conveyance. The usual and proper way to do this is to make a purchase money bond and mortgage, and put it on record within sixty days of its date, as required by the act of 1820. But in the English chancery, the doctrine of vendor's lien is sustained, not on the footing of a contract, express or implied, but avowedly independent of the contract, " upon the doctrine of the court," as Lord Eldon said, as an implied trust.

Exactly what words are sufficient to make such a contract, of course depends upon the construction of the instrument before the court. If, in the deed of conveyance of the property, it be expressly declared to be " under and subject to the payment " of a certain sum, part of the purchase money, there can be no doubt that the parties meant to charge

---

[1] *Semple* v. *Burd*, 7 S. & R. 285; *Hepburn* v. *Snyder*, 3 Barr, 72 ; *Zentmyer* v. *Mittower*, 5 Barr, 403.

the land with the payment of the money. They do so, by express words in the chain of the title, in such a way that a purchaser must come to a knowledge of it, if he looks, as he is bound to do, to see where his vendor got the property.[1]

But it is well settled that the charge must be *by express words*. Enough must appear upon the face of the deed of conveyance to enable the court to say that it was the contract of the parties that the unpaid purchase money should remain a lien. In *Bear* v. *Whisler*,[2] the deed of conveyance was in the usual form, and after the concluding words " In witness whereof, &c.," there was written " Subject, nevertheless, to the conditions and obligations contained in a certain article of agreement, &c." The agreement was recorded. It was held that there was an express charge of the purchase money mentioned in the agreement, and that the estate conveyed by the deed was an estate upon condition that the vendee should perform the agreement. In *Neas's Appeal*,[3] a deed came up for construction which had the words of charge in the premises, where the consideration is usually expressed, " in consideration of one thousand dollars, one hundred dollars whereof are to be paid annually to the grantor, until the whole be paid." It was held to create a lien. This case certainly comes within the line, and should

---

[1] *Heist* v. *Baker*, 13 Wr. 9; *Barnitz* v. *Smith*, 1 W. & S. 142.
[2] 7 Watts, 146.   [3] 7 Cas. 293.

have been decided the other way. There was nothing beyond a recital that the purchase money was unpaid, and no appearance of a contract that it should remain a lien until paid It was practically overruled in *Hiester* v. *Green*,[1] where a widow, by deed-poll, released her life estate in her husband's land "in the consideration of the payment to me yearly of the sum of one hundred dollars." It was held that she had no lien upon the land for the payment of the annuity. The opinion of the court discusses the authorities at some length, and reaches this conclusion from them.

"The sum of the authorities is, that though
" equitable liens are not favored by our law, yet
"parties may, by *express and clear* words, in deeds
" of conveyance, create liens upon land either for
" purchase money or for performance of collateral
" conditions, which will be binding between them-
" selves and their privies, and such liens will be
" divested by sheriff's sales, unless they are in the
" nature of testamentary provisions, or are not
" capable of valuation, or are expressly created to
" run with the land. Now in view of this state of
" the law, our immediate question is, whether reciting
" on the face of the title that the purchase money
" remains unpaid, and is to be paid annually,
" creates such a lien. In *Neas's Appeal*, an intention
" to create a lien was inferred from the fact that

---

[1] 12 Wright, 96.

"the purchase money stood in the title. But
"according to all the antecedent cases, express
"words were necessary to establish the lien. It
"never before was treated as a subject for legal
"implication, and it is manifestly a hazardous infer-
"ence to make; for the pecuniary consideration,
"essential to all bargains and sales, is generally
"mentioned upon the face of the deed, and if it
"be said to be unpaid, it is notice of *that fact* to
"a purchaser, but it is no notice to him of a lien.
"He may reasonably infer that the vendor trusted
"the personal credit of the vendee for the purchase
"money, or took bonds and mortgages, or other
"security, or at the least, that no lien was intended
"to be created by the deed, because none was ex-
"pressed. These inferences would seem quite as
"reasonable as that the parties meant what they
"did not express—a lien for the unpaid purchase
"money. When the evil consequences of con-
"structive liens are considered, and it is observed
"how the legislature and the courts have laboured
"to furnish record notice of liens, it is going very
"far to say that parties may, even by their express
"agreement, create a valid lien; but much too far
"to imply a lien from mere notice of non-payment
"of the purchase money. * * * * * * If
"notice of unpaid purchase money be sufficient to
"create a lien, *Kauffelt* v. *Bower* ought to have
"been differently ruled, for the purshaser there

"had such notice; but the court refused, for the "most solid reasons, to imply a lien."

To sum up on this subject then:—Where a vendor claims to have a lien for his unpaid purchase money upon the land which he has sold *and conveyed*, he must affirmatively show that he has expressly stipulated for it, either by a debt of record as a judgment or a mortgage duly recorded, or by an express agreement to that effect in the deed by which he has conveyed the title to his vendee. And if his lien is preserved by judgment or mortgage, he must comply with the statutory requirements with respect to record; for a judgment for purchase money has no priority over other judgments, but ranks with them according to the date of its entry.[1] And although a mortgage for purchase money has, by statute, a lien for sixty days without record, yet to get the benefit of the statute, its provisions must be strictly complied with.

LIEN BEFORE CONVEYANCE.—But before conveyance of the legal title—while there is nothing more than an agreement to convey—the case is entirely different. In such circumstances, the vendee has title only in equity, and the legal estate in the land remains in the vendor. Consequently, if the purchaser be in possession, the vendor may oust him,

---

[1] *Stephen's Executor's Appeal*, 3 Wright, 9.

and recover the land in ejectment on his legal title, if the purchase money be not paid.

The vendor is not in want of any aid from a court of equity. He has at law a complete remedy. But the title of a vendee under articles is only and purely equitable, and needs the support of equitable principles to exist even, and the maxim, "he who seeks equity must do equity," applies to him in full force. If he needs the protection of a court of equity to defend him against the legal title, as he certainly does, he must do equity by paying the price which he agreed to pay. And it is also clear that a purchaser from the vendee stands in precisely the same position. Even if he buys without actual notice of the unpaid purchase money, he buys only an equity, and although his equity be as meritorious as that of the vendor, between equal equities the law must prevail. Besides, there is warrant for saying that the very fact that a man has only an equitable, and not a legal title, is sufficient to put a purchaser from him, upon inquiry; and inquiry, duly pursued, would inevitably lead to notice of the reason why the conveyance of the legal title was withheld; that is, that the purchase money remained unpaid. So that even in the absence of actual notice, this would be sufficient to charge a person with *constructive* notice, and thus take away his equity altogether.[1]

---

[1] *Stokley* v. *Trout*, 3 Watts, 163; *Watson* v. *Willard*, 9 Barr, 89.

LIENS SUBSEQUENT TO CONTRACT.

LIENS SUBSEQUENT TO CONTRACT.—We come now to the consideration of those liens which attach to the land articled subsequently to the date of the contract. It is another singular result of our mixed system of law and equity in Pennsylvania, that so far as the statutory provisions for the liens of judgments, and for recording conveyances and other writings are concerned, that both the vendor and the vendee are deemed to have estates in the land.

JUDGMENTS AGAINST VENDOR.—A judgment against the vendor binds his interest in the land, and a judgment against the vendee binds his interest. If the vendor convey, the purchaser from him must record his deed, and so also if the vendee convey, the purchaser from him must record his deed. And all the doctrines with respect to notice which spring from these statutes apply with equal force to the estate of either. So far then as the judgment creditors of the *vendor* are concerned the contract of sale does not work an equitable conversion of his real estate into personalty.

If it were so, the judgments would not be liens on his property, for judgments do not bind personalty; but, notwithstanding the contract, the judgments against the vendor are liens on his estate in the land, and they may be enforced against it by execution, as against real estate; that is to say, by levy, condemnation, and sheriff's sale on *venditioni exponas*.[1] On such a sheriff's sale, the sheriff's vendee stands precisely in the situation of the original vendor. He is entitled to the legal estate of the vendor, to the unpaid purchase money, and to all the remedies for its recovery which the original vendor would have had.[2] It is therefore necessary for a vendee under articles to search for judgments against the vendor, up to the very delivery of the deed consummating the contract.

ATTACHMENT EXECUTION WILL NOT LIE.—It is a necessary consequence of this doctrine that although the unpaid purchase money is a debt due by the vendee to the vendor, yet it cannot, like other debts, be made the subject of an attachment execution.[3] If it could be so attached there would be little use in giving liens to judgment creditors of the vendor, for it would be possible that a junior judgment, by an attachment, might obtain priority over those who had been more vigilant than himself. The fact that judgments rank as liens, according to the date of their entry, means—if it means anything—that they are to be paid in their order, from the proceeds of the land when sold; and this would be impossible, if the unpaid purchase money could be reached by an attachment, as a debt.

---

[1] *Fasholt* v. *Reed*, 16 Sergeant & Rawle, 266.
[2] *McMullin* v. *Wenner*, 16 S. & R. 18.
[3] *Stewart* v. *Coder*, 1 Jones, 90.

LIENS SUBSEQUENT TO CONTRACT.

EQUITABLE CONVERSION IN OTHER CASES.—As a contrast to this let me direct your attention to the consequences of equitable conversion in other cases: that, for instance, of land, produced by a positive direction to sell contained in a will, such a direction as makes it the duty of the executor to convert the land into money, and, therefore, upon the theory that I have explained, equity will look upon the land as already converted, and upon the shares of those who have interest in the land, as personal estate. In such a case a judgment against the devisee of a beneficial interest in the land has no lien upon his share; neither can such a share be taken into execution and sold.[1] The purchaser at a sheriff's sale, under an execution levied upon such a share, acquires no title whatever, either to the land or its proceeds.[2] Indeed so logically is the doctrine of equitable conversion pursued to its conclusion in such a case, that it has been held, that where a testator, by his will, gave binding instructions to his executor to sell his land, the land may be taken in execution on a judgment obtained against the testator in his lifetime, and sold by the sheriff, without the *sci. fa.* to the widow and devisees expressly required by the statute, before such executions can issue.[3] This decision was rested upon the express ground, that because the testator had ordered his land sold, and therefore the interest

---

[1] *Morrow* v. *Brenizer*, 2 Rawle, 185; *Evan's Appeal*, 13 P. F. Sm. 183.
[2] *Brolasky* v. *Gally*, 1 P. F. Sm. 509.
[3] *Leiper* v. *Thomson*, 10 P. F. Sm. 177.

of the devisees was personal property, and not real estate, it did not come within the letter of the statute, which required such notice to be given before "the real estate of the widow, or devisees, or heirs," could be sold.

The vendor, also, may mortgage or convey his interest as real estate, and such mortgage or conveyance will be entirely sufficient, if the ordinary rules of law are complied with, to pass whatever remaining interest he may possess, without any such delivery, or change of possession, or notice, as is required to pass title to personal property or to a chose in action.[1]

EJECTMENT BY VENDOR.—The vendor may bring an ejectment upon his title against the purchaser in possession if the purchase money or all of it be not paid; for, as I remarked a moment ago, the vendee is not entitled to the protection of the equitable doctrine until he has done equity himself, by paying the price agreed upon. In so far then as is necessary to give the vendor a complete security, the doctrine of equitable conversion affords no protection to the vendee, but just as in England, a Court of Equity would, by injunction, interfere to prevent the vendor from proceeding with his ejectment, if the purchase money remaining due should be tendered to him in full, with interest; so our courts in Pennsylvania, while there was no chancery here, administered the equity

[1] *Leiper* v. *Irvine*, 2 Casey, 54.

of the vendee, and the vendor's action of ejectment would be arrested by the payment of the debt with interest, or a tender of the money; or even if that should not be done before the verdict was reached, his verdict in the ejectment would be conditioned to become void upon the payment of the balance due within a stipulated time.

SHERIFF'S SALE.—Of course, a sheriff's sale of the vendor's interest, under a judgment against him, would discharge all the liens upon that interest, but only those would be discharged which became liens upon his estate subsequent to the articles, and the purchaser at such a sale would take subject to the liens which existed upon the property at the time the contract was made. They would be unaffected by the sale, because their lien covered and bound the whole estate, both legal and equitable, in the land; and after such a sale the vendee's interest, and all the liens upon it, would remain precisely as they were before, entirely unaffected by the proceeding.[1]

JUDGMENT AGAINST VENDEE.—I have already said judgments against the vendee bind his equitable estate in the land. This was a necessary result of the system of giving equitable relief by means of common law forms. As Chief Justice Tilghman said, in *Auwerther* v. *Mathiot*,[2] "at common law an "equitable estate is not bound by a judgment or

[1] *Patterson's Estate*, 1 Casey, 71.   [2] 9 S. & R. 402.

"subject to an execution, but the creditor may have relief in chancery. We have no Court of Chancery, and have, therefore, from necessity, established it as a principle that both judgments and executions have an immediate operation upon equitable estates." But neither the lien of a judgment against the vendee, nor a sheriff's sale upon execution under such a judgment, could in any way affect either the legal estate of the vendor, his right to the purchase money, the liens upon his estate, or the liens upon the land prior to the contract. So that a purchaser at a sheriff's sale under such a judgment, would take precisely the same estate in the land which the vendee himself had; that is, an equitable estate subject to the payment of the unpaid purchase money, but discharged of all liens against the vendee himself, which would ordinarily be discharged by a sheriff's sale of his property.

MERGER.—A few words now as to the effect of the merger of the legal and equitable estates upon the various classes of liens about which I have been speaking. When the contract of sale is consummated by a conveyance, the legal and equitable estates, of course, merge and unite in the grantee, and therefore, after liens against the *vendor*, subsequent to the articles, have attached, the purchaser should not pay the vendor the balance of the purchase money and take a deed from him, for the judgments against the vendor will attach to the completed title in the hands of the vendee, because it was his folly to pay, without first seeing that the liens were satisfied. If there be judgments which are liens upon the estate of the *vendee*, and during their existence as liens, he acquires the legal title by taking a deed from the vendor, these judgments, which at their inception were liens upon the equitable interests of the vendee only, become liens upon the legal and equitable estates which have thus been merged into one. Now, in such a case, suppose the whole purchase money be not paid at the time of the conveyance, and the vendor take a judgment or a mortgage to secure the balance due, it is manifest that his judgment or mortgage, although immediately recorded, will be subsequent in point of *time* to those liens which have already attached to the vendee's equitable interest; yet because they were for purchase money which had, as such, a lien on the vendee's equitable interest, from the date of the contract, and therefore prior in that respect to the judgments against the vendee;—they will take precedence of such judgments as liens upon the vendee's completed estate. And it is no hardship to the judgment creditors of the vendee, that this priority, which had always existed, should be continued. Besides, it might be said that, as to judgments against the vendee, the legal title thus subsequently acquired should be considered as after-acquired property, which, as judgments, they could not bind. But in order to secure this priority it is incumbent upon the vendor that he shall diligently enter his judgment, or record his mortgage as soon as the conveyance is made. In one case where the vendor took a judgment bond as security for the unpaid purchase money upon making a deed, on which bond judgment was entered in his favor one hour after the conveyance, it was held that such a judgment took precedence of prior judgments against the vendee, which bound his equitable estate only.[1] And in another case it was held, with respect to a mortgage, that where the vendor, on making conveyance of the legal title, took a purchase money mortgage as security for the balance due at time, his mortgage would take precedence of prior judgments against the vendee, if, according to the act of 1820, it was recorded within sixty days from its date. If not so recorded the opportunity was gone, and the prior judgments took precedence of it.[2] This peculiar doctrine was well illustrated in the recent case of *Taylor* v. *Preston*.[3] Preston bought land from Young for $21,000 and paid $5,200 on account. He then assigned all his estate in the land to Taylor, at which time, two instalments of the purchase money due Young, amounting to $15,800, remained unpaid. When one of these instalments came due, Young brought an action of covenant against Preston for the money, whereupon

---

[1] *Love* v. *Jones*, 4 Watts, 465.
[2] *Academy* v. *Frieze*, 2 Watts, 16; *Foster's Appeal*, 3 Barr, 30.
[3] 29 P. F. S. 440.

Preston confessed judgment to Young for the whole of the balance with interest, and took a deed from Young for the land. The court held that Preston had no title whatever, except the title of a trustee. He held the legal title subject to the lien of Young's judgment, the whole equitable estate in the land having passed by his assignment to Taylor; and upon payment of the balance of the purchase money remaining due, which in effect would be nothing more than payment of Young's judgment against Preston, a conveyance from Preston to Taylor could be enforced:—and subsequent judgments against Preston were no liens upon the land, because there was nothing, either of title or possession in him, which the judgments could possibly bind.

IV. THE EFFECT OF A SHERIFF'S SALE OF THE LAND WHICH HAS BEEN ARTICLED, UPON THE TITLE, AND UPON LIENS.

Of course, the results of such a sale would depend very much upon the kind of lien under which it was made, whether upon a lien *prior to the contract*, or upon a proceeding by the vendor to enforce payment of the *unpaid purchase money*, or a subsequent judgment against the vendor, or a judgment against the *vendee* subsequent to the contract.

SALE ON LIEN PRIOR TO CONTRACT.—If the sale were made on a lien prior to the contract, it would be the right of the execution creditor to have his money out of the land, as it was when his lien attached upon it; and the purchaser from the sheriff would take the title as it existed in the vendor at the time the lien attached. Consequently such a sale would entirely cut out all the rights of both vendor and vendee under the contract; and all the liens subsequently attaching upon the interests both of the vendor and the vendee would be transferred to the purchase money in the hands of the sheriff. When the rights of subsequent lien creditors to the proceeds of the sheriff's sale came to be considered, it would be found that each would be paid out of so much of the proceeds as could fairly be considered to represent the estate in the land which was bound by his lien. For instance, a judgment against the vendor, obtained subsequently to the articles, would be paid out of so much of the proceeds as would be necessary to pay the balance of the unpaid purchase money due the vendor, and if that balance should be exhausted before the judgment was fully satisfied, of course, the remainder of the judgment could not be paid, for neither the vendor, nor any one claiming in his right subsequent to the date of the contract, could reasonably expect to have more from the proceeds of the sale than the unpaid purchase money. Any further interest in the land would belong to the vendee, and those claiming under him, as representing his equitable interest. The liens against the vendee's interest, subsequent to the contract, would not be paid at all, until so much of the proceeds as was necessary to fully satisfy the unpaid purchase money should be set aside and disposed of. The balance, be it great or small, would be applicable to the liens against the vendee, or if there be none, would belong to the vendee himself.[1] And it would make no difference whatever, whether the amount thus paid to the vendee, or those claiming in his right, be greater than the amount of the purchase money already paid by him, for if the land have increased

[1] *Siter's Appeal*, 2 Cas. 178; *Crouse's Appeal*, 4 Cas. 139.

in value since the contract to such an extent that it will produce at a sale a price greater than that stipulated for in the contract, the advantage belongs entirely to the vendee, because after the contract is made, he is to this extent, in equity, the owner of the land, that any loss or profit arising from it, equally belongs to him. If the land increase in value, it is his gain. If it decrease, or if improvements be destroyed by fire or otherwise, it is his loss.[1]

SALE ON PROCEEDING FOR PURCHASE MONEY.—Where the land is sold upon a proceeding by the vendor to enforce payment of the unpaid purchase money, the purchaser from the sheriff will take both the legal and the equitable title, as it stood in the vendor at the time the contract of sale was made. If the vendor himself should buy at such a sheriff's sale, it amounts to a rescission of the contract, and he is disabled thereafter from making any further claims upon the vendee.[2] The idea was advanced in *Wilson v. Stoxe*,[3] that upon such a sale only the vendee's interest would pass to the sheriff's purchaser, because the execution should be levied, not on the fee, but upon the equitable estate of the vendee, for no man willingly sells his own estate on his own execution. But this idea was negatived in *Horbach v. Riley*,[4]

---

[1] *Stevens' Appeal*, 8 W. & S. 186; *Kerchall v. Day*, 2 Harris, 112; *Robb v. Mann*, 1 Jones, 300; *Morris v. Rice*, 7 Watts, 437.
[2] *Day v. Lowrie*, 5 Watts, 412. [3] 10 Watts, 434. [4] 7 Barr, 81.

which has been subsequently affirmed in many decisions,[1] and it was settled, as I have said, that the purchaser from the sheriff takes the whole estate, legal as well as equitable. The proceeds of such a sale go to the vendor to the extent of his unpaid purchase money, without any regard whatever to the date of his judgment under which the sale is made. The legal title which he held, and which passes to the purchaser by the sheriff's sale, was a security in his hands for the whole of the unpaid purchase money, and it is upon the strength of this, and not because of any lien which his judgment might have, that he is entitled to priority of payment.[2] If anything remains after the vendor is paid in full, it belongs to the vendee, for the money, standing in the place of the land, is to be divided according to the respective interests of the parties in the land.

SALE ON JUDGMENT AGAINST VENDOR.—Where the sheriff's sale takes place upon a judgment against the vendor subsequent to the contract, no liens are discharged except those which attached to his interest subsequent to the contract, and the purchaser takes the position of the vendor; that is, has his legal estate and his right to the balance of the unpaid purchase money, subject to all the liens which existed at the time the contract was made,[3] for they are not

---

[1] *Vierheller's Appeal,* 12 Harris, 105; *Canon v. Campbell,* 10 Casey, 309; *Ziegler's Appeal,* 19 P. F. S. 471.
[2] *Vierheller's Appeal, supra.*   [3] *Patterson's Estate,* 1 Casey, 71.

discharged by the sheriff's sale. In distributing the proceeds of such a sale, of course, nothing is paid but those liens which are discharged, and if there should be a surplus it would belong to the vendor himself.

SALE ON JUDGMENT AGAINST VENDEE.—In like manner a sheriff's sale of the land upon a judgment obtained against the vendee, subsequent to the contract, discharges only those judgments which are liens upon his equitable interest. A purchaser takes the equitable title subject to the payment of the unpaid purchase money, and liable also to all the liens which existed before the date of the contract; and the proceeds of such a sale would be distributed only among the judgment creditors of the vendee who had liens upon his equitable interest, and if there be any surplus it would belong to the vendee.

v. THE REMEDY UPON THE CONTRACT.

That may be either by a *bill* for specific performance, by an *action of ejectment*, or by *action upon the contract* for its breach.

BILL FOR SPECIFIC RELIEF.—I have already mentioned the general principles upon which the Courts of Equity proceed in the enforcing of specific performance of contracts for the sale of lands, and how that remedy differs from the redress afforded by a common law court under like circumstances. It must be remembered, however, that specific performance is a matter of grace, and not of right, and the chancellor, if he finds reasons to withhold his assistance, will refuse specific performance and leave the party to his remedy by an action at law for damages. It must affirmatively appear that the contract is *valid and binding*, it must be *certain and capable of being enforced*, it must be *fair and equitable* and upon *sufficient consideration*, and the *plaintiff must show that he has done*, or is ready to do, all that is required upon his part. What I have to say on the subject of the contract being binding and certain was said at the last lecture, and I will not recapitulate it now. With regard to the contract being one capable of being enforced, that is, equivalent to saying that the court will not make a vain decree which cannot be obeyed. Thus, if a man agrees to sell real estate to which he has no title whatever, it would be absurd to say that he shall complete that contract by conveying the estate to his vendee. It is impracticable and cannot be enforced.

DOWER.—Let me illustrate this by a case of somewhat frequent occurrence. This rule is applied to the case of an agreement by a married man, to sell and convey his estate in land, where his wife refuses to join in the deed of conveyance. It was at one time the rule in equity that the court would enforce the performance of such an agreement by a process of contempt against the husband, until he exerted his authority over his wife, or until her acquiescence should be extorted by affection or fear; but it has long been settled that equity will not decree specific performance of the contract under such circumstances; for it was found that in some cases the imprisonment of the husband was not such a hardship to the wife as to induce her to part with her rights; and besides, it would be a mockery to procure the conveyance of the wife, in a manner sufficient to bar her dower, by exerting such a constraint upon her, and at the same time to require her to acknowledge solemnly that she executed the deed of her own free will and accord, and without any coercion or compulsion by her husband, as required by the statute.[1] The vendee may recover damages for the breach of such a con-

---

[1] *Clark* v. *Seirer*, 7 Watts, 107; *Weller* v. *Weyand*, 2 Grant, 103.

tract in an action at law, however, for the husband ought not to have made a contract which he proved unable to fulfil.

It is well settled that the court will not enforce an unwilling purchaser to take a doubtful or unmarketable title, yet if the seller have any title at all, and the purchaser wishes to have it and pay for it, such as it is, it must be conveyed to him; for it would be unjust to allow the seller to take advantage of his own wrong, or default, or misdescription. Therefore, where the title or the property so far falls short of that agreed for, that the court would not compel the purchaser to take it, *the choice rests with him* to take it or not, or to have so much of the agreement performed as the seller can perform, and to have an abatement out of the purchase money, or a compensation in some way for the deficiency in title, quality, quantity, or other matter, where the seller's ability to perform falls short of his contract. But not in every case will the court allow such rebate. It is only where it is just and equitable to do so, and where it can be done without making any material alteration of the contract, as the parties intended it. Otherwise the decree might, in effect, make a new contract for the parties—one which, perhaps, they would not have made for themselves. Thus, in a case where a bill was filed to enforce a contract by a married man to sell land, and his wife refused to join in the deed, the Court of Common

Pleas referred the cause to a master, to report what abatement from the price, or change in the terms, should be made. The master reported that forty per cent. of the purchase money should remain on mortgage, as a security to the vendee against the possibility of the wife surviving her husband and claiming dower; but the Supreme Court reversed the decree, and dismissed the bill on the ground that the wife's refusal to join in the deed was a bar to specific performance at all, unless the vendee was willing to take the husband's deed alone, and pay the whole price. If he did not choose to do so, he must be left to his remedy in an action for damages.[1]

If however, the vendee is willing to pay the whole price agreed, and take such title as the vendor can give,—that is, subject to the wife's dower,—the court will make a decree to that effect.[2] Therefore as a matter of practice, if a conveyancer or lawyer wishes to draw a contract for a sale of land by a husband, in such a way as to render a purchaser secure of getting the title, he must have the contract executed and separately acknowledged by the wife also, in the same manner that her deeds are required by the statute to be acknowledged, and then the court will decree specific performance by both husband and wife.[3] Such an acknowledgement will avail for a contract of

---

[1] *Reisz's Appeal*, 23 P. F. Smith, 485.
[2] *Burke's Appeal*, 25 P. F. Smith, 141.
[3] *Dankell* v. *Hunter*, 11 P. F. Smith, 382.

sale of the land, whether it belongs to the husband or to the wife, but without that acknowledgment the courts will not interfere.[1] If the vendor should die without executing the contract, and the vendee should pursue the remedy for specific performance prescribed by the acts of assembly to enforce contracts of decedents, the decree authorized by the statute, whether it be made by the Orphans' Court or by the Court of Common Pleas, will not carry the property to the purchaser clear of the wife's dower. In no way can her dower in her husband's land be divested, without her consent, except upon an execution against her husband, or a sale for the payment of his debts.[2]

MUTUALITY.—Moreover, the contract must be *fair and equitable*, and upon sufficient consideration. It must be manifest that no unfair advantage has been taken, and no trick or undue influence exerted, in making the contract. For, as the granting of a decree is of grace and not of right, there are many cases in which a plaintiff could recover damages at law for the breach of a contract, upon which he has no standing whatever in a court of equity. In such cases the bill is dismissed without prejudice, that is, without so far determining the question of right as to make the decree a bar to an action as *rem adjudicatam*. A contract is not fair unless it is mutually binding, and it is a cardinal principle that

---

[1] *Roseburg* v. *Sterling*, 3 Casey, 392.
[2] *Riddlesberger* v. *Mentzer*, 7 Watts, 141.

a chancellor, when uncontrolled by arbitrary enactment, executes no contract which is not the source of mutual obligation and mutual remedy. Thus, as I said in the last lecture, a contract, wholly verbal, for the sale of land, cannot be enforced against the vendor, because of the statute of frauds—neither can he recover the purchase money against the vendee, because that would be to allow him to enforce a contract which he need not keep unless he chooses, and which is totally devoid of mutuality.

MARKETABLE TITLE.—*The plaintiff must show that he has done*, or is ready to do, all that is justly required on his part. He must be able to show that he has a marketable title which is beyond reasonable uncertainty.[1] "It has been well and " wisely settled," says Judge Sharswood, "that under " a contract for the sale of real estate the vendee has " the right to have conveyed to him, not merely a " good, but an indubitable title. Only such a title is " deemed marketable, for otherwise the purchaser " may be buying a law suit, which will be a very " serious loss to him, both of time and money, even " if he ultimately succeeds."[2] In a court of law the question is whether the title is good or bad. The distinction between a good title and a marketable title is peculiar to a court of equity.[3] But what is

---

[1] *Swain* v. *Fidelity Insurance Company*, 4 P. F. Sm. 455.
[2] *Swayne* v. *Lyon*, 17 P. F. Sm. 439.
[3] *Nicol* v. *Carr*, 11 Casey, 381.

a marketable title, is a very difficult definition to give. In *Dalzell* v. *Crawford*,[1] — a case always referred to on this question—Judge King stated, as the result of the equity doctrine, that no title will be forced upon an unwilling purchaser if he is able to raise any question of law or fact, which may appear to a judge sitting in equity, so doubtful that a title involving it ought not to be enforced. The doubts, however, which will operate on a cour of equity are not doubts made up for the occasion, not based on captious, frivolous and astute niceties, but such as produce real *bona fide* hesitation in the mind of the chancellor. The doubts must be considerable and rational, such as would and ought to induce a prudent man to pause and hesitate in the acceptance of title.[2]

A vendor who is unable to give possession without probable litigation, is not in position to ask for specific performance, and he is left to his remedy at law for a breach of contract,[3] or, where there is a single contract for the sale of several pieces of property, and the contract is entire, a failure of title to a part of property, or to one piece, is a bar to specific performance of the contract as to the remainder, if the purchaser be unwilling.[4]

COMPENSATION.—There are cases where the court

---

[1] 1 Parsons, 46; 1 Clark's L. J. Rep. 155.
[2] *Anschutz* v. *Miller*, 2 Weekly Notes, 547.
[3] *Dech's Appeal*, 7 P. F. Smith, 467.
[4] *Finley* v. *Aiken*, 1 Grant, 83; *Freetly* v. *Barnhart*, 1 P. F. Smith, 279.

will grant specific performance with compensation, as it is called;—where the plaintiff is not able to show a strict compliance with his agreement, and therefore could not recover on the contract in a court of law. But such decree will be made only where the deficiencies are of little importance, and in no case where the defect is in a matter which formed an inducement to the purchase.

TIME NOT MATERIAL.—The most frequent occasion for its exercise occurs in cases where the plaintiff has not come up to the requirement of his contract with respect to the time limited for its performance. At law time is material, and a failure in this respect is fatal to the claim of the party in default, but in equity time is not generally deemed to be of the essence of the contract, unless the parties have so expressly treated it, or it necessarily follows from the nature and circumstances of the contract.[1]

Of course, if the plaintiff has come short of his contract in respect of time, he must furnish a reasonable excuse. *Laches* are a bar to his claim, and in a suit for specific performance, as well as in every other proceeding in equity,—perhaps more than in any other—a stale claim is never favoured.[2] There is nothing to prevent parties from binding themselves as to the time of performance if they choose to do

---

[1] *Remington* v. *Irwin*, 2 Harris, 143.
[2] *Cadwalader's Appeal*, 7 P. F. Sm. 158; *Piersol* v. *Neill*, 13 P. F. Sm. 420.

so, and when they make such a contract, it will be strictly enforced.[1]

Where time is not of the essence of the contract a decree may be made against a purchaser, if the seller can make a good title at the time of the decree, unless there has been bad faith, or an improper speculation.[2] But a party cannot speculate upon a title which he does not own or control, and then ask for a decree for specific performance.[3]

BILL AGAINST PURCHASER.—While there can be no doubt that, in any case of a contract for the sale of real estate coming within the requirements that I have mentioned, a *vendee* would have the right to go into equity for specific performance, it cannot be said, under the decisions in Pennsylvania, that a *vendor* is entitled under all circumstances, to the same remedy. It is necessary that the vendee should have the means of compelling his vendor to make a conveyance to him on receipt of the purchase money, and as there is no proceeding, known to the common law, by which such a result can be reached, he will be without remedy unless he has relief in equity; where the chancellor's decree can accomplish precisely the result desired. But the vendee has promised only *to pay money*, and an action upon the contract for the purchase money, brought in a court of law, by the vendor against

---

[1] *Patchin* v. *Lamborn*, 7 Casey, 314.
[2] *Lay* v. *Huber*, 3 Watts, 367; *Tiernan* v. *Roland*, 3 Harris, 439.
[3] *Clark* v. *Vanatta*, 12 Harris, 257.

the vendee, is an entirely sufficient remedy in a great majority of cases.

This was the argument of the English Court of Exchequer in the old case of *Armiger* v. *Clark*,[1] decided in 1722, where the Chief Baron said, "if a "man comes for specific performance as *to land itself*, "a court of equity ought to carry it into execution, "because there is no remedy at law; but if it is "to have a performance *in payment of money*, "they may have a remedy for that at law." But the doctrine was not received with favour, and it was soon settled by the English chancellors that the vendor should have the same remedy by bill for specific performance as the purchaser—although the relief extended no further than the collection of a sum of money. This, not only because the action at law was not a remedy adequate to that of a bill in equity, but also upon the distinct ground that the remedy between the purchaser and the vendor should be mutual.[2]

When, in 1836, equity jurisdiction was conferred upon our courts by statute, they were expressly given power "to afford specific relief, when a recovery "in damages would be an inadequate remedy." Under this, there can be no question that it was the commonly received interpretation, that all cases where courts of equity enforced specific performance under equitable doctrines, were included, and

---

[1] Bunbury's Reports, 111.
[2] *Witting* v. *Cottal*, 1 Sim. & Stu. 174; *Adderly* v. *Dixon*, 1 Sim. & Stu. 607.

the report books of our courts furnish very many instances of bills brought by vendor against vendee to enforce payment of the purchase money, which were sustained without question.[1]

It is true that there was in Pennsylvania a large number of lawyers and judges, chiefly among the elders of the bar and bench, who were extremely hostile to the introduction of chancery forms of procedure, from the sincere belief that complete justice had been done and could be done under our Pennsylvania system. An able exposition of the views of that class of the profession is to be found in the dissenting opinion of Judge Black, read in the case I have last mentioned. "I may as well confess myself," said he, "to be among those " who are steadfastly opposed to any extension " whatever of the chancery powers, except where " it is manifestly necessary to prevent a failure of " justice. I think it was not an ignorant prejudice, " but high political wisdom which caused our " ancestors to refuse a court of chancery any " place among their judicial institutions. The men " who founded this commonwealth, built up her " reputation, achieved her liberties, and settled her " land, knew very well the amount of good and " evil which such a court had done elsewhere, and " upon sound and deliberate judgment they re- " pudiated it as far as they could. The administra- " tion of law, blended and mixed with the equity

---

[1] *Dalzell* v. *Crawford*, 1 Pars. 37; *Finley* v. *Aikin*, 1 Grant, 83.

"principles, was a happy conception. It is no
"bungling substitute, but a most admirable improve-
"ment of both legal and chancery practice. There
"never was any natural reason for separating
"justice from law or law from justice, and it was
"emphatically right to break down the artificial wall
"of partition, which certain professional interests
"had built up between them in the mother country.
"Some of the states of this Union, after a full
"trial of chancery, have imitated our example.
"Others are rapidly preparing to do so, and even
"English reform has gone far in the same direction.
"It is to be fervently hoped that we will not now
"extinguish the light by which the world has been
"walking. The right of trial by jury needs no
"vindication. It is necessary, if for nothing else, to
"check the tendency of the judicial mind to run
"into a metaphysical refinement. The two elements
"of a legal tribunal, the learning of the one, and
"the practical common sense of the other, have a
"most salutary influence upon the judgments which
"both most concur in pronouncing. No mode of
"ascertaining truth can be infallible, but with a jury
"that scorns all subtle evasions of plain justice,
"and a judge who frowns upon vulgar prejudices,
"we come as near the right as any system can
"come in this world. To that mode of trial we
"owe one mighty fact, viz.: that wherever it pre-
"vails, lawyers, with an influence always powerful
"and often preponderant, are the steady defenders

" of rational, regulated, constitutional liberty, instead
" of being, what they are elsewhere, the mere tools
" of oppression." Upon the direct question involved,
Judge Black further says, using precisely the reasoning in *Armiger* v. *Clark*,[1] "every bill for specific
" performance—this one like the rest—prays for
" relief on the express ground that the plaintiff
" has no remedy at law. Is the fact true in this
" case? Assuming every averment of the bill to
" be correct, and the whole answer to be false,
" would not an action at law have given the plaintiff
" full, complete, and ample redress? Certainly it
" would. He asks for nothing but money. The
" ultimate object of every word in the decree is to
" 'put money in his purse.' Will it be pretended
" that a court and jury cannot give him as much
" money as he ought to have? If justice to either
" party requires the verdict to be coupled with
" conditions, has not all experience demonstrated
" that such conditions can be easily and safely
" imposed? Cannot a legal tribunal determine how
" many dollars and cents will compensate a vendor
" of real estate for any breach of the contract, as
" easily as it can ascertain the amount due on a
" promissory note or a book account? The truth
" is that this party, so far from being remediless at
" law, has an unusual variety of remedies by action,
" all of them cheap, easy, simple, certain and com-
" plete. He may bring suit for the first instalment.

[1] *Supra*, page 56.

"Retaining the title in his own hands, as a pledge (literally a mortgage) for the balance, he can demand, when it becomes due, either that the land shall be given up to him or sold to satisfy him. In case he sees proper to keep the land and sue on the broken covenant for damages merely, he can recover as much as will make him altogether whole. If the purchase money agreed on was more than the value of the property, or if the price has fallen in the meantime, he can recover the whole difference, together with full compensation for all his expense, disappointment and trouble. In either of these ways he would have the benefit of every equitable principle which a chancellor could administer. He did not come— he could not have come—into equity, because the law was defective, for the truth is otherwise." This quotation is from a dissenting opinion, agreed to by two judges out of five; the majority of the court having decided the other way.

The difference between the English and the Pennsylvania rule (with regard to the jurisdiction of a Court of Equity to entertain a bill against the purchaser to compel payment of the purchase money by him) was fully asserted by the Supreme Court in *Kauffman's Appeal*,[1] where, as euphemistically stated by the reporter, "*Finley* v. *Aiken*, was *examined*," and the doctrine was squarely asserted by Justice Agnew, that, where nothing more is sought

[1] 5 P. F. Sm. 383.

by the bill than the payment of the purchase money, the court will not entertain it, but will leave the plaintiff to his remedy by an action at law. And this was affirmed in *Dech's Appeal*,[1] where the same judge used the following language: " Here the " plaintiff has a complete and adequate remedy " upon his covenant. He only seeks *to recover his* " *money*, and this he can easily do by an action, if " he have fulfilled his own part of the contract. We " have said, in a case decided at Harrisburg (*Kauff-* " *man's Appeal*), that where there is nothing whatever " in the circumstances of the case requiring the aid " of chancery to give effect to the contract, and the " bill for specific performance is simply an action, " and nothing more, to recover purchase money, we " will not entertain it. The decree in such case " being of grace merely, and the party having a " full and adequate remedy at law, we will not lend " the strong arm of chancery, armed with the power " to arrest the body for contempt, to enforce the " payment of a mere debt from which the body is " exempt under the non-imprisonment law."

The reasoning of Judge Black in *Finley* v. *Aiken* was in opposition to the general current of authority on the question of equity jurisdiction, both at the time his opinion was delivered, and since.[2] If the courts could proceed according to equity forms,

---

[1] 7 P. F. Sm. 467.
[2] *Kirkpatrick* v. *McDonald*, 1 Jones 393; *Yard* v. *Patton*, 1 Harris 281; *Stephens* v. *Forsyth*, 2 Har. 68; *Wistar* v. *McManes*, 4 P. F. Sm. 328; *Unangst's Appeal*, 5 P. F. Sm. 138.

only where the plaintiff had no remedy according to common law forms in this State, the equity jurisdiction would have been a very narrow one indeed, for equitable principles had been so long a part of our common law, and the forms of proceedings in our courts had been so moulded to allow of their enforcement, that there remained very little that could not be accomplished, in the way of giving relief, without resorting to a bill in equity. It was held by Chief Justice Gibson, as early as 1849,[1] that the extension of the remedy by actions at law, to cases originally within the jurisdiction of equity, and particularly the system adopted in Pennsylvania of administering equitable relief through the medium of common law forms, is no bar to the equitable jurisdiction of the courts for the same cause.

It is difficult to see any good reason why the decision of the Supreme Court in *Finley* v. *Aiken* should have been practically overruled, as it has been. That decision was in harmony with the English cases, and there existed the same grounds here as there, why the remedy in equity should be mutually open to both parties. The reason given in the able opinion in *Dech's Appeal*,[2] seems to me to be insufficient, viz.; that chancery might enforce a decree for payment of the purchase money, by an arrest for contempt. The act of 1842, forbidding imprisonment for debt, expressly prohibits the arrest of any person

---

[1] *Wesleyan Church* v. *Moore*, 10 Barr, 274.   [2] *Supra*, page 61.

for the payment of money under a decree founded on contract; and the opinion of the profession on the application of that statute is fairly shown by the opinion of Judge King in the case of *Hugg, et al.*,[1] where he decided that a defendant cannot be taken in execution by process, either in equity or at law, where the decree is for the payment of money founded on contract.

I think it might safely be asserted that a very large number of cases could be found in the reports of the Supreme Court, where such bills by vendors against vendees have been filed and decrees made upon them without question, but the safer plan for a practitioner to adopt is to bring his action for the purchase money, in all cases where it can be maintained.[2]

But after these decisions it cannot be affirmed that, as a general rule in this State, a bill in equity will lie against a purchaser to enforce payment of the purchase money; and perhaps it would be venturing too far, and would amount only to a conjecture, if I were to undertake to define exactly the limits of this equitable jurisdiction. Generally speaking, in order to entitle a vendor to maintain a bill, there must be some failure on his part to observe the minor or less important stipulations of the contract, which a court of equity would excuse, but which

---

[1] 1 Clark's L. J. Rep. 154.
[2] *Speakman* v. *Forepaugh*, 8 Wright, 363; *McBride* v. *Smyth*, 4 P. F. Sm. 245; *Nicholson* v. *Bettle*, 7 P. F. Sm. 384; *Doebler's Appeal*, 14 P. F. Sm. 9; *Swain* v. *Fidelity Co.*, 4 P. F. Sm. 455; *Womrath* v. *McCormick*, 1 P. F. Sm. 504.

might seriously affect his remedy in a common law action; or there must be some act to be done by the purchaser, more than the mere payment of money, which is sought to be enforced by the decree. If there be such, it seems that his bill may be maintained, otherwise an objection to the jurisdiction is fatal.

EQUITABLE EJECTMENT.—The circumstance which I have so frequently mentioned, that for a hundred years we administered equity through common law forms in Pennsylvania, gave rise to another remedy, which, during that period, was very commonly used to enforce specific performance of contracts with respect to real estate. That is the action of *equitable ejectment*. If the vendor, after the articles, remained in possession of the land, there was no other method for the vendee to adopt to enforce specific performance, than to pay or tender the purchase money in full, and bring an action of ejectment to recover the possession upon his equitable title, and in all cases where a court of equity in England would enforce specific performance upon a bill, a court of common law in Pennsylvania can direct a verdict for the plaintiff in ejectment, and thus allow him to enforce his equity by the recovery of possession. The same remedy also was used in cases where, under the articles, the vendee went into possession, leaving the legal title outstanding in the vendor, as security for the unpaid purchase money. The vendor had his choice either to bring an action of debt or covenant upon his articles for the money, or to bring an action of ejectment to recover possession of the land, which could only be defeated by the payment of the balance due. Of course the remedy by ejectment would naturally be the most effectual, for it would give him the land back again, unless his money was paid, without going to the expense and trouble of a sheriff's sale, and the delay in getting possession by that means.

EJECTMENT SUBSTITUTE FOR BILL.—By means of conditional verdicts, the common law action of ejectment was so moulded as to do complete justice between the parties, and to form a good practical substitute for the remedy by bill. It was said by Judge Huston, in 1840, that "greatly more than half our " ejectments are of this description."[1]

How completely our courts succeeded in giving to an equitable ejectment all the substantial incidents of a suit in equity may be seen from a cursory view of the authorities. The judge trying such a cause is a chancellor, and as Judge Sharswood said in a recent case, " the jury are merely his assessors, to assist " him upon the credibility of witnesses, and in " reconciling conflicting testimony."[2] The relative duties of judge and jury are entirely different from those devolving on them in ordinary common law

[1] *Seitzinger* v. *Ridgway*, 9 Watts, 507. [2] *Robinson* v. *Buck*, 21 P. F. Sm. 391.

actions. The conscience of the chancellor must be satisfied, for it is he, and not the jury, who is charged with administering the equities of the case. The judge controls the decision, and if the case of the plaintiff be, in his opinion, one which would not move a chancellor to decree a specific performance, or to grant relief, he must withdraw the case from the jury and give them binding instructions to find for the defendant; if the case on the testimony should be sufficient to entitle the plaintiff to relief, then he should so instruct the jury and leave them to find whether the evidence be true or not. C. J. Gibson likens an equitable ejectment to the trial of an issue directed by a chancellor to find the facts, in ease of his conscience.[1] The chancellor is not bound by the verdict, but may direct any number of new trials, or decide in opposition to the verdict. And although the court cannot give judgment in ejectment against the verdict, yet it will and ought to set it aside, unless the case is clearly a suitable one for equitable interposition.[2]

The conferring of equitable powers to decree specific performance by bill has not taken away from our courts anything of the jurisdiction they possessed to afford the same relief through common law forms. This has been decided so often as to need no reference to authority. It has been a favorite method of administering justice with our courts. In *Church*

---

[1] *Brawdy* v. *Brawdy*, 7 Barr, 158.
[2] *Piersoll* v. *Neill*, 13 P. F. Sm. 420; *Miller* v. *Henlan*, 1 P. F. Sm. 265.

v. *Ruland*,[1] it was argued by counsel that the equitable ejectment was merely a substitute adopted from necessity to enforce equities, at a time when that could not be done in the regular way; and now that the courts could give relief by bill, the equitable action ought to be considered as obsolete. But the court referred to the numerous cases, since the act of 1836, in which equitable ejectments had been maintained, and in which the same question had been decided, and then continued:

" Nor is such an administration of equity justly
" open to the reproaches cast upon it in the oral
" argument in this case. It is not the substitution
" of twelve unlearned chancellors for a lawyer pre-
" pared for his office by the lucubrations of twenty
" years. The judge in reality is the chancellor with
" the assistance of a jury. It is not like ordinary
" trials at law, where any evidence, reasonably tend
" ing to prove a fact, must be submitted to be
" passed upon by that tribunal. The conscience of
" the judge, as chancellor, must be satisfied, and
" what goes to the jury is to determine the credibility
" of the witnesses, and to weigh and decide upon
" the force and effect of conflicting testimony. What
" is this but the trial of a feigned issue out of
" chancery? If the evidence is too vague, uncertain
" or doubtful to establish the equity set up, even if
" believed, it is the duty of the judge to withdraw

[1] 14 P. F. Sm 441.

" it from the jury, either by a nonsuit, or a binding direction in his charge, as the case may require."

CONDITIONAL VERDICT.—The method by which the equities are administered in this mode of proceeding,—is—as has been said—a conditional verdict, by which the jury, under instructions from the court, find a verdict and annex it to certain conditions or qualifications which are to be satisfied and fulfilled before the successful party is entitled to its benefit.

As applied to cases arising on contracts of sale, such conditions usually are for the payment of money within a specified time. If the vendee be in possession, and the ejectment be brought by vendor to enforce payment of the unpaid purchase money, the verdict would usually be for plaintiff, to be released if the defendant pay the balance within a given time. If the vendor be in possession, suit being by vendee to enforce specific performance, the verdict would be for plaintiff, to become void if balance should not be paid.[1]

A time within which the payment is to be made must always be fixed by the verdict, and a judgment on a verdict defective in this respect is erroneous and will be reversed.[2]

The time for payment fixed by the verdict is of the essence of the finding, and a failure to pay on

[1] *Hill* v. *Oliphant*, 5 Wright, 374.
[2] *Thompson* v. *McKinley*, 11 Wright, 353.

or before the day amounts to a rescission of the contract and is conclusive upon the rights of the parties.[1]

And in this respect the plaintiff, if he be bound to any payment by the conditions of the verdict, is as liable to lose its benefit as the defendant. A vendee seeking specific performance in ejectment, must pay the balance of the purchase money found by the verdict to be due, within the limited period, or he is concluded by the verdict and his equity to the land is gone.[2]

After the verdict and judgment the whole matter is in the hands of the court. The time of payment may be enlarged, or the money may be ordered into court to await the making of proper conveyances.[3] And if the vendor can make title only to an undivided part of the property sold, the vendee may elect to take such part and will be required to pay only the proportional part of the purchase money. If he has paid the whole purchase money into court, he will be allowed to take out the surplus after paying for so much of the property as can be conveyed to him.[4]

ONE JUDGMENT ENOUGH.—The ordinary rule established by statute in regard to the conclusiveness of a verdict and judgment, is that it requires two

---

[1] Act of 21 April, 1846, Purdon, p. 535, sec 18; *Treaster* v. *Fleisher*, 7 W. & S. 137; *Hewitt* v. *Huling*, 1 Jones, 35.
[2] *Hill* v. *Oliphant*, 5 Wright, 374.
[3] *Webster* v. *Webster*, 3 P. F. Sm. 161.
[4] *Erwin* v. *Myers*, 10 Wr. 96; *Napier* v. *Darlington*, 20 P. F. Sm. 64.

verdicts and judgments the same way, to settle the questions of title involved in the cause, between the parties; either two in succession, or two out of three. At common law, ejectment only determines the right of possession, and a verdict and judgment are not conclusive upon the title; so that an unsuccessful party who has lost one action might begin another, and so on indefinitely. Equity, however, interposed by injunction after repeated trials all having the same result, to stop further vexation of the successful party, and to quiet his possession. In the celebrated case of the *Earl of Bath* v. *Sherwin*,[1] the chancellor was applied to, to put a stop to a litigation based on the alleged illegitimacy of a certain Duke of Albemarle, which had lasted through two generations, during which time five actions of ejectment had been tried, all resulting in favor of the plaintiff in chancery. Lord Cowper dismissed the bill, but the House of Lords on appeal reversed the chancellors decree and ordered an injunction. This established the equitable jurisdiction, and it has not since been questioned. The rule was afterwards settled that, after three verdicts in ejectment the same way, the court would interpose to put an end to the litigation, and as early as 1795, this was adopted by the Supreme Court of Pennsylvania.[2] The jury found a verdict for the plaintiff without leaving the box. C. J. McKean then told the

---

[1] 4 Bro. Parl. Cas. 373.   [2] *Cherry* v. *Robinson*, 1 Yea. 521.

defendant that four different juries had united in opinion concerning the title. It was high time, he said, that peace should be restored between them; but if he still meant to contest the right, and worry his adversary out, courts of justice would interfere and prevent him from dragging his opponent into further vexatious law suits. As equity would decree an injunction after three trials, so would our courts stay further proceeding by their summary powers for the ends of justice.

The act of 1807, finally fixed the limit to the number of ejectments, as I have already stated.

But the provisions of this act do not apply to equitable ejectment at all. After a decree for specific performance in chancery there could be no second trial, and as the judgment in equitable ejectment is the substitute for, and equivalent to, a decree, consequently, one verdict and judgment in equitable ejectment is a bar to further proceedings upon the same equitable title, just as conclusively as a decree in equity for specific performance would be.[1]

This was decided in 1840, and in the following year the Legislature adopted a joint resolution, declaring that the act of 1807 should be construed to extend to all actions of ejectment, whether brought on legal or equitable title, or whether such action be brought as a substitute for a bill in equity, or for any other purpose. This changed the rule for the time being, but the resolutions were repealed by act of April 30th,

---

[1] *Seitzinger* v. *Ridgway*, 9 Watts, 496.

1850, and the law as declared in *Seitzinger* v. *Ridgway* was restored.[1]

There must be a judgment entered. A verdict without judgment is not enough.[2]

ACTION FOR BREACH OF THE CONTRACT.—The party who breaks his contract to buy or to sell real estate is liable to the other party in an action. Such actions differ from other actions upon contracts, chiefly, I may say only, in two important particulars. One of these—the kind of evidence required—I have already considered. The other difference is in the measure of damages, which is the last subject that I will touch upon.

MEASURE OF DAMAGES.—It will be impossible for me, in the brief time allowed, to discuss, even superficially, the huge volume of conflicting and contrary decisions on this vexed question to be found in the English and American report books. I can only indicate generally how the law now stands.

Damages are sought on such contracts on two occasions—when the vendor refuses to convey, and when the vendee refuses to pay.

DAMAGES AGAINST VENDOR.—The measure of damages in suits against the vendor, when he refuses or is unable to convey, depends upon the position he

---

[1] *Peterman* v. *Huling*, 7 Cas. 432.
[2] *Ferguson* v. *Staver*, 4 Wr. 213.

occupies in the transaction. It was determined long ago in England, that where the vendor is *unable* to convey a good title, and is not guilty of any fraud, the purchaser cannot have any compensation for the loss of his bargain; but the damages must be confined to the money paid, with interest, and actual expenses incurred by the plaintiff.[1]

This was an exception to the general rule as to damages for breach of a contract of sale, which is that the seller must pay the difference between the contract price and the market value of the article at the time when it should be delivered.[2] Consequently, where the vendor was able to convey and refused, or where he acted fraudulently in making the bargain, the general rule was applied, and the disappointed vendee might recover not only the money he was out of pocket on the transaction, but compensation for the profit he would have made had the vendor dealt fairly with him.[3]

The reason of the distinction taken was stated by Sir William Blackstone to be that contracts for the sale of real estate "are merely upon conditions, "frequently expressed, but always implied, that the "vendor has a good title." But this remark is fairly open to criticism, for, as was said by Lord Hatherly in a recent case, "if the vendor's contract was *on the* "*condition* that he had a good title, then, in the event

---

[1] *Flureau* v. *Thornhill*, 2 W. Bl. 1078.
[2] *White* v. *Tompkins*, 2 P. F. Sm. 363.
[3] *Wall* v. *The Real Property Co.*, L. R. 9, Q. B. 249.

" of the title failing, there would be no action for dam-
" ages whatever; and there would be no power in
" the vendee to do that which he is always entitled
" in equity to do, namely, to insist upon having the
" title, good or bad, if he should be so minded."[1]

The doctrine of *Flureau* v. *Thornhill*, has, however, been recently fully established in England, and subsequent cases qualifying it have been overruled.[1]

And the same doctrine has been adopted by our own Supreme Court.[2] The question, therefore, in an action against a vendor, is whether he is honestly unable to convey, or whether he is fraudulently seeking to avoid a bad bargain. If he has acted with good faith he can be compelled to pay only actual damages suffered by the vendee; but if he has been guilty of collusion, tort, artifice, or fraud, it is otherwise, and compensation for the loss of the bargain may be added.

DAMAGES ON VERBAL CONTRACT.—Let me advert now to what I said in the last lecture about the Statute of Frauds—that the fourth section of the British statute is not in force here, and, therefore, an action may be brought for the breach of a parol contract for the sale of land. In this respect, it has been said with regret, the law of Pennsylvania differs from that of every other State in the Union.[3] The

---

[1] *Bain* v. *Fothergill*, L. R. 6 Exch, 59; L. R. 7 H. L. Cas. 158.
[2] *Bitner* v. *Brough*, 1 Jones, 127; *McClowry* v. *Croghan*, 7 Cas. 22.
[3] *Ewing* v. *Thompson*, 16 P. F. Sm. 382.

result has been a great deal of litigation, and a conflicting and contradictory series of decisions which cannot be reconciled.

I may mention, in passing, that the circumstance that a Court of Equity has refused to enforce a verbal contract, is no bar to a subsequent action to recover damages for its breach.[1]

The general rule, as now established, is that the damages to be recovered for breach of a verbal contract must not be such as to amount to an enforcement of performance of the contract. As Justice Woodward said in a leading case,[2] " such actions were
" rare in the early history of our jurisprudence ; and
" when they were brought, the measure of damages,
" though not very distinctly defined in the cases,
" was so controlled that specific performance of the
" contract should not be virtually enforced. It is
" too manifest for debate, that if the value of the
" land may be recovered in an action of case upon
" the *parol* contract, the statute, as we have it, is
" as effectually evaded as if the land itself were
" recovered in ejectment. Therefore it was, that
" whilst the personal action was sustained, because
" forbidden by nothing in our statute, the damages
" recovered were measured by other standards than
" the value of the land at the time of the recovery.
" In some of the early cases, it would seem, the
" damages were merely nominal ; in none were they

---

[1] *Poorman* v. *Kilgore*, 1 Wr. 309.
[2] *Hertzog* v. *Hertzog*, 10 Cas. 418.

"more than compensatory of what had been paid on the footing of the contract."

This most notable exception to this rule, arose in a class of cases (now overruled) where an owner of land had verbally agreed to convey or devise land in consideration of services to be performed for him in his life time. It was held that such contracts were not for the sale of land, but for services to be paid for in land, and consequently they were not within the ban of the statute; and that the measure of damages is not the value of the services but the value of the land.[1]

These decisions, it was truly and forcibly remarked, "placed the value of all the real estate in Pennsylvania at the mercy of parol evidence in its most unsatisfactory and dangerous form,"[2] and they have been overruled, as I have said. The law is now settled, by many subsequent decisions, and may be formulated thus:

1. An action on verbal contract cannot be maintained for the purchase money, but damages for the breach may be recovered.[3]

2. Where the consideration is paid by the vendee in services, the measure of damages is the value of the services and not the value of the land.[4]

---

[1] *Jack* v. *McKee*, 9 Barr, 235; *Bash* v. *Bash*, 9 id, 260; *Oyer* v. *McDowell*, 9 Har. 417; *Malaun* v. *Ammon*, 1 Grant, 123.

[2] Dissenting opinion of Woodward J., in *Malaun* v. *Ammon*, 1 Grant, 149.

[3] *Wilson* v. *Clarke*, 1 W. & S. 554.

[4] *Hertzog* v. *Hertzog*, 10 Cas. 418; *Dumars* v. *Miller*, 10 Cas. 319; *Ewing* v. *Thompson*, 16 P. F. Sm. 382.

3. The measure of damages in other cases, is the money actually spent, or expenses incurred, by vendee, including improvements made, on the faith of the contract, deducting rents, if he has had possession; and *not* including the value of the bargain unless the vendor has been guilty of fraud.[1]

4. Where the vendor has been guilty of fraud, the vendee may recover for the loss of his bargain, although the suit be on a verbal contract.[2]

5. But a mere breach of the contract, by a refusal to convey, is not fraud in this sense, even though the vendor has title and power.[3]

DAMAGES AGAINST VENDEE.—Upon the vendee's refusal to pay, the action against him will be either to recover the purchase money with interest, or— considering the contract at an end — to recover damages for his refusal to take the land at the price agreed on. For, of course, the future ownership of the land depends upon the position taken by the vendor as plaintiff. If by his action he recovers the price, his right to the land is gone, and he is but a trustee for the vendee, if he still holds the title. This should always be made apparent upon the record, either by the pleadings, or in some other manner; although if the question be afterwards raised, it is competent to show by oral testimony

---

[1] *Bender* v. *Bender*, 1 Wright, 419; *McNair* v. *Compton*, 11 Cas. 23.
[2] *McNair* v. *Compton*, supra; *Meason* v. *Kaine*, 17 P. F. Sm. 126.
[3] *Harris* v. *Harris*, 20 P. F. Sm. 170; *Thompson* v. *Sheplar*, 22 P. F. Sm. 160; *Ruckert* v. *Domenec*, 2 Weekly Notes, 195.

exactly what was tried and concluded by the verdict.[1]

Where the contract is a binding one, under the statute of frauds, there is usually no reason why the general rule which applies to all actions for the breach of a promise to pay money should not operate, namely, that the measure of damages is the sum promised to be paid, with interest from the time when payment should have been made.[2]

If, however, suit be brought for damages arising from the refusal, and not for the purchase money, the measure of damages is the same as that on breach of contract for the sale of a chattel, that is the difference between the contract price, and the diminished value of the land at the time the contract ought to have been executed. The difference may be ascertained either by a re-sale at auction, or in any other fair way satisfactory to the jury, and any special damages the vendor may have sustained may be added to the verdict.[3]

I have already considered the question of damages on a verbal contract as fully as time will admit.

INTEREST. — The general rule with respect to interest upon purchase money, in the absence of any express stipulation about it, is that where the

---

[1] *Erie Gas Co.* v. *Haverstick*, 6 P. F. Sm. 28.
[2] *Tripp* v. *Bishop*, 6 P. F. Sm. 424.
[3] Sedgwick on Dam. (6th ed.) 222–3; *Ashcom* v. *Smith*, 2 Pen. & W. 219; *Tompkins* v. *Haas*, 2 Barr, 75; *Baney* v. *Killmer*, 1 id. 30; *Bowser* v. *Cessna*, 12 P. F. Sm. 148.

vendee is in possession he pays interest, and otherwise not, for in the one case he is receiving the profits of the land, if any, and in the other case the vendor, receiving the profits, ought not to be entitled to claim interest.[1] There are cases, however, where this rule is not applied.[2]

LIMITATION.—It only remains to notice the limitation imposed on such suits or actions by the 6th section of the act of April 22d, 1856,[3] which enacts that no rights of entry shall accrue, or action be maintained, for a specific performance of any contract for the sale of any real estate, or for damages for non-compliance with any such contract * * but within five years after such contract was made, * * unless such contract shall give a longer time for its performance, or there has been in part a substantial performance, or such contract * * shall have been acknowledged, by writing, to subsist by the party to be charged therewith, within the same period.

But the statute does not run against a vendee so long as he is in possession of the land sold.[4]

In conclusion I wish only to remind you that I have, as it were, merely sketched the outlines of a field which you must go over in detail ; and I trust that I

---

[1] *R. R. Co.* v. *Cooper*, 8 P. F. Sm. 408; *Cox* v. *Henry*, 8 Cas. 18.
[2] *Tyson* v. *Passmore*, 2 Barr, 122 ; *McCormick* v. *Crall*, 6 Watts, 207 ; *Kester* v. *Rockel*, 2 W. & S. 365.
[3] Purdon, 930, pl. 14.
[4] *Webster* v. *Webster*, 3 P. F. Sm. 161.

may have at least awakened your interest in this important subject, the careful study of which will so amply repay you.

INDEX.

ACKNOWLEDGMENT.
    A contract by a married woman must be separately acknowledged by her,   52

ACTION
    will lie for breach of verbal contract,   12
    for breach of contract,   74
    (See *Damages.*)
    Limitation of actions on such contracts,   81

ATTACHMENT EXECUTION
    will not lie for unpaid purchase money as a debt due vendor,   36

BARGAIN. (See *Measure of Damages.*)

BILL. (See *Specific Performance.*)
    Remedy by bill for specific performance,   49, 66
    What plaintiff must aver and prove,   49
    Where vendor is a married man and his wife refuses to join in conveyance,   50
    sometimes dismissed without prejudice,   53
    Such decree no bar to subsequent action,   77
    for purchase money only cannot be maintained,   56, 65

BREACH OF CONTRACT.
    Difference between law and equity,   5

CHANGE OF POSSESSION
    is necessary to take verbal contract out of statute of frauds,   18

COMPENSATION.
    Specific performance with compensation sometimes decreed,   51, 55

CONDITIONAL VERDICT. (See *Ejectment.*)

CONTRACT. (See *Breach, Measure of Damages, Mutuality, Statute of Frauds.*)
    Requisites of contract for sale of land,   9, 20
    Vendor must sign. Vendee need not,   12
    Form of contract not at all material,   13
    Seal not necessary, .   14
    must contain all the essential elements,   15
    No words of inheritance necessary,   16
    (See *Executory Contract.*)
    Effect of contract for sale of land,   21
    must be valid and binding, .   49
    capable of being enforced,   49
    must be fair and equitable,   53
    must be performed by plaintiff,   54
    Time not usually of the essence of the contract,   56
    Damages for breach of the contract, .   76
CONVERSION. (See *Equitable Conversion.*)
    What legal conversion is, .   21
CONVEYANCE
    ordinarily destroys vendor's lien, . . .   28
    Effect where wife refuses to join in conveyance,   50–2
    Purchase money may be ordered into court to await conveyance, .   71

DAMAGES. (See *Measure of Damages.*)
    may be recovered for breach of parol contract, though specific performance be forbidden,   12
DECEDENT.
    Verbal contract of decedent provided for by statute, .   18
    Where the contract of a decedent is enforced the dower of his widow is not barred, . . .   53
DEVISEE
    of vendee is entitled to have the land paid for from testator's estate, ...   25
DISTRIBUTION
    of proceeds of sheriff's sale of land which is under contract, .   36, 39, 45, 47, 48
DOWER.
    Where the wife of vendor refuses to join in conveyance no decree will be made, . .   50

DOWER.—*Continued.*
    Unless the purchaser is willing to take subject to her
        dower, and pay full price, ... 51-2
    Contract by husband and wife, separately acknowledged,
        will be enforced against both, ... 52
    not barred by decree to carry out contract of decedent, 53

EJECTMENT
    brought to enforce specific performance, . . . 66
    may be maintained in all cases where a chancellor would
        grant relief, ... 66
    may be brought by either party against the other in pos-
        session, ... 67
    by vendor to collect purchase money, . . . 38, 67
    Substitute for bill, ... 68
    Functions of judge and jury in equitable ejectment, . 68
    Conditional verdict in ejectment, ... 70
    Time of payment must be fixed in verdict, . . 70
    Time of payment is material, and both parties are bound
        by it, ... 71
    Time of payment may be enlarged by court, . . 71
    Money may be ordered into court, ... 71
    One verdict and judgment conclusive, . . . 73
    Origin of rule as to number of verdicts stated, . . 71-3

ELECTION.
    Where title is unmarketable, the purchaser may elect
        whether to take or not, ... 51

EQUITABLE CONVERSION.
    The doctrine stated, ... 21
    Is a fiction, ... 21
    Not extended to lien creditors of vendor, subsequent to
        contract, ... 35
    How applied in cases other than those arising on con-
        tracts of sale, ... 37

EQUITABLE EJECTMENT. (See *Ejectment.*)

EQUITY. (See *Fraud, Part Performance, Specific Perform-
        ance, Words of Inheritance, Time.*)
    View taken of breach of contract, ... 5
    Courts of equity bound by statutes, ... 17
    No courts of equity in Pennsylvania from 1736 to 1836, 8
    System in Pennsylvania considered, . . . 58, 64
    restrains vexatious litigation in ejectment, . . 72

EXECUTORY CONTRACT.
 Words of inheritance not necessary; in an executed contract they are, ... 16

FEE. (See *Executory Contract*.)
FORM OF CONTRACT
 under Statute of Frauds, ... 14
 No form necessary, ... 14
 Must contain essential elements of contract, . . 15
FRAUD (See *Statute of Frauds*.)
 by vendor changes the measure of damages, which may be recovered against him, ... 75, 79

HEIR
 or devisee of vendee entitled to have land paid for from his estate, ... 25
HUSBAND. (See *Dower*.)

INHERITANCE.
 Words of, not necessary in executory contract, . 16
INJUNCTION
 against vendee, from cutting timber, . . 24
INTEREST.
 When allowed on purchase money, . . 80

JUDGMENT (See *Liens*.)
 against vendor, subsequent to contract, binds his estate in the land, ... 36
 The same, against vendee, ... 36
 Attachment execution on judgment against vendor, will not lie for unpaid purchase money, . . . 36
 against vendee binds his equitable estate only, subject to the purchase money, ... 39
 against vendor—Sheriff's sale on, ... 47
 against vendee—Sheriff's sale on, . . . 48
JURISDICTION
 in equity to decree against purchaser, . . 57
 in ejectment not repealed by statute, . . . 68
 in equity and at law concurrent in some cases, . 64

INDEX. 87

JURY.
    Part performance not a question for, . . . 20
    in equitable ejectment, judges of fact only, . . 67

LACHES
    a bar to decree for specific performance, . 56

LIENS (See *Judgment.*)
    prior to the contract are unaffected by the contract, . 26
    And are not discharged by a sheriff's sale, on a judgment subsequent to the contract, ... 39
    created by the contract. (See *Vendor's Lien.*)
    subsequent to contract, may be upon estate either of vendor or vendee, ... 35
    of judgments against vendor, subsequent to contract, bind his estate only, and the same as to vendee, . 35
    of judgments subsequent to contract, discharged by sheriff's sale of the interest they bind, . . . 39
    How proceeds of sheriff's sales are distributed among lien creditors, ... 36, 39, 45, 47, 48

LIMITATION
    of actions, on contract of sale of real estate to five years, ... 81
    Statute does not run against a vendee in possession, . 81

LOSS OF BARGAIN. (See *Measure of Damages.*)

MARKETABLE TITLE (See *Election.*)
    distinguished from "good" title, ... 54
    must be free from reasonable doubt, . . . 55
    where possession cannot be delivered, the title is not marketable, ... 55
    The title must be marketable at the time of the decree, 57

MARRIED WOMAN. (See *Dower.*)

MEASURE OF DAMAGES
    in suits against vendor depends upon whether he has been guilty of fraud, ... 75
    If he has, or refuses to convey, the damages may include loss of bargain, ... 76
    on verbal contract, ... 12, 76, 79
    must not amount to enforcement of the contract, . 77
    Where consideration is the services of the vendee, the measure is the value of the services, not the value of the land, ... 78

INDEX.

MEASURE OF DAMAGES.—*Continued.*
    The rule stated, ... 78–9
    in suits against vendee, ... 79
    When interest on the purchase money should be
        allowed, ... 80

MERGER
    of legal and equitable estates by conveyance, . 40
    Effect of merger on liens, . . 41

MORTGAGE.
    The title of vendor, after contract, is like that of a
        mortgagee, ... 24

MUTUALITY
    is necessary to the validity of contract, . . . 13
    A verbal contract is not binding on purchaser for want
        of mutuality, ... 54

PARTITION.
    A vendee in possession may maintain partition against a
        co-tenant of his vendor, ... 25

PAYMENT.
    Time of. (See *Ejectment.*)

PART PERFORMANCE
    What it is, . . . 17
    Change of possession indispensable, . 18
    The change must be *after* contract, . 19
    And in pursuance of it, . . 19
    Possession taken must be exclusive, 19
    And co-extensive with the contract, 20
    not a question for a jury, . 20

POSSESSION. (See *Part Performance.*)

PURCHASE MONEY
    a lien before conveyance, 23, 33
    (See *Vendor's Lien.*)
    cannot be attached as a debt due to vendor, . 36
    Sheriff's sale on proceeding for, ... 46
    Bill for purchase money only cannot be maintained, . 57–65
    may be ordered into court on a conditional verdict, . 71
    Interest on purchase money, ... 80

PURCHASER (See *Vendee.*)
    from vendee, before conveyance, takes subject to lien for
        purchase money, ... 34

PURCHASER.—*Continued.*
    from sheriff. (See *Sheriff's Sales.*)
    may choose whether he will take an unmarketable
        title, ... 51
    Bill against purchaser cannot be maintained if for
        money only, ... 57, 65

QUESTION OF LAW.
    Whether part performance has been made out, . . 20
    The judge administers the equities in equitable ejectment, 67

REAL ESTATE. (See *Equitable Conversion.*)
REMEDY (See *Action, Bill, Ejectment, Equity, Specific Performance.*)
    ought to be mutual, ... 64

SHERIFF'S SALE
    on lien prior to contract passes title clear of the con-
        tract, ... 26, 44
    on judgment against vendor subsequent to the contract, 35
    in cases of equitable conversion under wills, . . 37
    on judgment against vendee subsequent to contract, dis-
        charges only liens on estate of vendee, . . . 40
    on lien prior to contract; title of purchaser, . . 44
    Distribution of proceeds, ... 45, 47, 48
    on proceeding for purchase money passes whole estate
        in the land, ... 46
    on judgment against vendor, subsequent to contract,
        passes his estate only, ... 47
    on judgment against vendee passes only equitable estate,
        subject to lien for unpaid purchase money, . . 48
SPECIFIC PERFORMANCE (See *Bill, Ejectment, Laches.*)
    General principles, ... 5
    not applicable to sales of chattels, ... 7
    applicable to all sales of land, . . . 7
    of parol sales forbidden, ... 12
    Bill for, what plaintiff must show, ... 49
        (See *Bill.*)
    with compensation; when decreed, . . 51–55
    by Ejectment, (See *Ejectment.*) . . . 66–74

STATUTE OF FRAUDS.
    Statement of, . . . , . . . 9
    Pennsylvania statute, ... 11
    (See *Contract.*)
    Verbal contract binding under Pennsylvania statute, although specific performance is forbidden, . . 12
    Exception, (See *Part Performance.*) . . . 17

SURVEY
    Ordered by court to ascertain boundaries, . . 15

TENANT IN COMMON
    in possession cannot sell by verbal contract to his co-tenant in possession, ... 19

TIMBER.
    Vendee restrained from cutting timber before payment of purchase money, ... 24

TIME (See *Ejectment, Laches.*)
    not material in equity, but may be made so by express contract, ... 56

TITLE PAPERS.
    Possession of them was a badge of a good title in England, ... 28

VENDEE (See *Judgment, Purchaser.*)
    need not sign contract, ... 13
    in equity is owner of the land sold, ... 23
    Vendee's title not altered by non-payment of purchase money, ... 23
    restrained by injunction from waste, ... 24
    in possession may maintain partition, . . . 25
    Damages in suits against vendee, ... 79

VENDOR
    must sign contract of sale, ... 12
    at law is owner after contract, ... 21
    in equity holds legal title as security only, . . 23
    Vendor's position resembles mortgagee, . . . 24
    Liens against vendor, subsequent to contract, . . 35, 45
    (See *Judgments.*)
    after contract may mortgage or convey his title as real estate, ... 38
    may bring ejectment on his legal title, . . . 38
    Damages in action against vendor, ... 74

VENDOR'S LIEN
    arises from the contract itself, . . . 26
    English doctrine stated, ... 27
    repudiated in Pennsylvania, ... 28
    Generally conveyance destroys lien for purchase money, 28
    Express contract for lien may be made in conveyance, 29
    Express words necessary, ... 29
    Mere recital that purchase money is not paid will not suffice, ... 31
    Before conveyance the vendor holds legal title as security for purchase money, ... 33

VERDICT. (See *Ejectment.*)

WASTE.
    Vendee in possession must not commit waste, so as to diminish security for the unpaid purchase money, . 24

WIFE. (See *Dower.*)

WORDS OF INHERITANCE. (See *Executory Contract.*)

The Publishers are indebted to ALFRED I. PHILLIPS, ESQ., for kind assistance in preparing this Index.

---

www.ingramcontent.com/pod-product-compliance
Lightning Source LLC
Chambersburg PA
CBHW020302090426
42735CB00009B/1180